Practical Vedanta

Spirituality – Social Welfare – World Peace

Science and religion will meet and shake hands.

– SWAMI VIVEKANANDA

Other Books by the Same Authors

1. The Social Role of the Gita: How and Why
2. The Social Message of the Gita Symbolized as Lokasamgraha
3. तुलसी रामायण – जगमंगल-परायण
4. मानस एवं गीता – लोकमंगल-गुञ्जिता
5. लोकसंग्रहसन्देश:
6. The Gita and Tulsi-Ramayana: Their Common Call for the Good of All
7. Selections from the Mahabharata
8. The Gita for the 21st Century
9. छात्रोपयोगी भगवद्गीता
10. श्रीमद्भागवत का ज्ञान
11. The World Peace Agenda
12. Apad-Dharma in the Mahabharata
13. The Social Message of Mahayana Buddhism
14. Anu-Gita in the Mahabharata
15. Practical Vedanta Movement

Satya P. Agarwal

Urmila Agarwal

Including a Chapter by

Will Tuttle

PRACTICAL VEDANTA

Spirituality - Social Welfare - World Peace

Edited by

Seema Agarwal-Harding

New Age Books

New Delhi (India)

PRACTICAL VEDANTA

SPIRITUALITY - SOCIAL WELFARE - WORLD PEACE

ISBN: 978-81-7822-375-9

First Indian Edition: Delhi, 2017

Published by
NEW AGE BOOKS
A-44 Naraina Industrial Area, Phase-I
New Delhi (India)- 110028)
E-mail: nab@newagebooksindia.com
Website: www.newagebooksindia.com

Library of Congress Cataloging-in-Publication Data
Agarwal, Satya P./Agarwal, Urmila
ISBN 978-81-7822-375-9
Includes Introduction, Foreword,
Hinduism

Printed and published by
RP Jain for NAB Printing Unit
A-44, Naraina Industrial Area
Phase-I, New Delhi-110028. India

This book presents Practical Vedanta as the Spiritual Revolution of the modern age for the good of the world. The book is in two parts. Part I summarizes the pioneering work of Vivekananda–Tilak–Aurobindo–Tagore–Gandhi–Tuttle, spread over the last 120 years. Part II is a simplified presentation of Practical Vedanta carrying the timely appeal, in Hindi and English – Arise, awake, move on from spirituality to social welfare, and stop not till you achieve world peace.

FOREWORD

I recall a poem my mother wrote two years ago, called "My Life is My Language."

My life is my language; there is no difference between the two
My laughter, words, moving around, or my daily tasks
They are the story of my life, and they mark my life
By giving offerings to others at the right occasion; eating together
Consider this as my offering of service to you all, and my joy
Whatever knowledge I have gained from God, I like to pass it on to you through my actions and these words
This is my age-old journey, and this is my life story
Whatever I am today is not from myself alone; I am a result of others' contributions
I am grateful to everyone from the bottom of my heart
And I give my love to everyone

This poem, or a "reflection" from my mother of her life, encapsulates her and who she is. In fact, it is a poignant reminder of who my parents are. This poem and hundreds of additional poems, written just like this one, by my mother Urmila, are contained here, in Part II of this book. They serve as a grateful reminder, a kind of beacon of light and hope for our family – a teaching from our mother to us on conducting oneself in life, as she conducted herself in her own life.

Part I outlines the foundation and development of Practical Vedanta, started by Vivekananda in 1896. Vivekananda's pursuit for creating a harmony between religion and science, coining the phrase "Practical Vedanta", was a desire to create a modern society where the spiritual and the secular would be combined harmoniously in a warm handshake between religion and science. Later writers, such as Tilak, Aurobindo, Tagore and Gandhi exemplify this thinking in their work, spreading the ideas of Practical

Vedanta beyond India to activists and writers such as Tuttle and my father.

I write this foreword to celebrate my parents' lifelong work, exemplified by their own lives and how they conducted it, inspired by the values of Practical Vedanta described in this book. I am struck by how much they have taught me, and the family. Most of all, they have taught us the meaning of love; love towards all, and the true meaning of dignity for all living beings.

The basic principle of human dignity as embodied in the United States Declaration of Independence encapsulates a fundamental aspiration shared by all humankind – the desire, first, to be loved as equals. It's a powerful paradigm that creates a lens through which to see the world around us. Can we truly love others equally as ourselves? Our parents teach us how it can be done.

Our paradigms - correct or incorrect - are the sources of our attitudes and behaviors, and ultimately our relationships with others. The term *paradigm shift* was introduced by Thomas Kuhn in his highly influential landmark book, *The Structure of Scientific Revolutions,* showing how almost every significant breakthrough in science is first a break with tradition, with old ways of thinking, with old paradigms.

In the realm of religion and philosophy, a break with old ways of thinking was accomplished by Swami Vivekananda, when he started the Practical Vedanta Movement in 1897.Vivekananda viewed Practical Vedanta as a way to update and make relevant ideas that have guided our spiritual journey from centuries ago, ensuring their relevance for the new scientific age.

Vivekananda's movement was strengthened by Tilak, Aurobindo, Tagore and Gandhi. More recent thinkers, such as Tuttle, are continuing with this movement forward into the 21st Century, with newer practical themes, such as love of all life manifested through a Vegan diet. Similarly, my father's work on *Lokasamgraha* – the Good of All – and Practical Vedanta is a reminder of the practical significance of ancient teachings from the Gita, Mahabharata and Ramayana for our everyday life and everyday work.

My parents, Satya and Urmila, have dedicated their lives to living by the values and principles of Vedanta, and have inspired us – their family – to also live by these spiritual values in support of social welfare and world peace. Their work on Practical Vedanta began early in life. I asked them the secret of their creative thinking so that we may glimpse at those moments in their lives that have helped shape their thinking, and in turn, teach us.In reply, they mention Gita/Anu-Gita's five favorable forces – God's grace, parental attention early in life, disciplined life-style free of greed and arrogance, pursuit of vegetarianism and the respect for all life forms, and love and support of family – especially one's children and grandchildren.

My parents' interpretation of the 'five favorable forces' guiding their own lives begins with "God's Grace", bringing them strength and fortitude. Mahatma Gandhi always said, "God is Truth", and that truth and non-violence go together in what can be described as "spontaneous adherence to divine principles", as advised by the Gita.

Foundations of "*karmayogins*" are laid early in life. Parental attention to living by divine principles – the second favorable force in my parents' lives—was laid by my grandparents, propelling them to live their lifelong journey by the values of social service and peace, manifested in their thinking and actions. "Karmayoga" is the yoga (discipline) of "karma" (action). Similar to the teachings of the Buddhist "middle path" – *Karmayoga* is the pursuit of action that demonstrates dedication without attachment, without greed, with humility, and with perseverance. The pursuit or life's journey is in taking action, not hankering after its reward. Moreover, action that is taken in pursuit of the "good of all" (*Lokasamgraha*) requires an unequivocal concentration, devoid of distractions from trappings of greed and success. This is the central teaching of the Gita, and the central value by which my parents try to conduct themselves as *karmayogins.*

My father was born in 1924, at Rajgarh, near Pilani in Rajasthan, which was at that time, a well-known center of education in India. My grandfather (Ram Swarup Agarwal) took a personal interest in the education of his children, believing that academic excellence would be their biggest asset going forward in life, especially as India emerged from under two hundred years of British rule. Education, and the value that his parents placed on it, became a gift my father received and has since passed on to us – his children and grandchildren.

As part of that education, and beyond exposure to modern thinking and new scientific knowledge, my grandfather also advocated for knowledge of Sanskrit. The knowledge and understanding of Sanskrit became instrumental in opening up a world of Indian scriptures and teachings, instilling in my father a deep regard for India's ancient spiritual teachings and culture. Sanskrit is the language of India's pre-eminent spiritual scriptures – the Gita, Mahabharata and Ramayana. Without the knowledge of Sanskrit, my father would have found it impossible to study India's ancient Hindu philosophy, and pass it on to us, interpreting their teachings and making them relevant to our contemporary world. My grandfather knew that without Sanskrit, any study of the Gita and its interpretations by modern social activists – such as Tilak and Gandhi—would be difficult.

My mother Urmila (Mital) Agarwal, was born in 1931 in Bareilly, Uttar Pradesh. At the time that she was born, her father was in an Indian jail, imprisoned by the British who were rulers of India at the time. Nanaji (my grandfather) was a prominent freedom fighter of his time, and the year was 1931. The "Free India Movement" was at its highest peak at that time, and processions were a commonality everywhere, even in my mother's hometown of Muzzaffarnagar in

Uttar Pradesh (UP). Most of the processions used to begin from her house.

Right from the time that my mother was born, Nanaji was a social activist, imprisoned numerous times by the British, for various reasons during India's freedom struggle. Because my mother was born while Nanaji was in jail, Naniji (my grandmother) stayed with her husband's brother in Bareilly at the time when she was born.

My mother tells us of the time when people who would come to the house, people close to the freedom struggle and lawyers. Almost anybody who was part of the freedom struggle was a lawyer at the time[1], including my two grandfathers. My maternal grandfather (Dwarka Prasad Mital) was a close ally of Gandhiji – the Father of the Nation, and Shastriji, the second Prime Minister of India, as well as Nehruji, our first Prime Minister. Numerous other prominent dignitaries of the time, who were preoccupied with the "Free India Movement", were close acquaintances of the family.

My mother learnt to love creative arts and crafts through her cousin Swarna, with whom she lived for three years as a child. From an early age, my mother's art work showed promise, as her teachers awarded her the highest awards for her art work when she was in school, and later in life she found ways to demonstrate her creative talents in public and prominent ways.

Together with her creative talents, my mother applied her leadership and managerial skills in various activities, such as when she was elected President of the Indian Women's Association, when my parents were posted to a country in Africa with the United Nations, or when she got a chance to show her leadership qualities and zeal for social service while

---

[1] My parents help us understand that the reason why there were so many Indian lawyers at that time, was that this was a "free" profession, not controlled by the British.

teaching arts and craft to students in Baltimore Temple for five years.

Among leadership qualities, my mother includes perseverance – her ability never to lose heart, no matter how difficult the circumstances. She draws inspiration from India's leaders such as Mahatma Gandhi, who pursued his non-violence movement for 28 years, believing "there is no such thing as defeat in the path of truth and non-violence"—a central teaching of the Gita.

My maternal grandfather, was a prominent follower of Mahatma Gandhi and my mother was the first person to garland Gandhiji as he alighted from the train when he visited Muzaffarnagar.

The search for newer challenges, with a fearlessness and ferocity for taking risk, and a determination to overcome hardship, has shaped our family from the time of our grandparents, propelled by the family's early migration from Mandawar (in Bijnor district, Uttar Pradesh, India). Migration due to marriage has been a common feature in women's lives in India and other parts of the world, and positive attitude towards migration for progress, became a common theme in my parents' life from an early age, when they were married. Some of India's leading industrialists, such as Birla, were migrants. Inspired by such leaders of the community, and national leaders such as Gandhi (who spent 21 years in South Africa perfecting the art of non-violent social resistance), my parents too were determined to embrace the challenges of migration and change. They have spent much of their adult life in "new" environments, without losing their spiritual connections with India and the teachings of Gita and Vedanta.

Our grandparents imparted strong leadership qualities in their children as well as a keen sense of social activism. My maternal grandmother, a prominent member of Kalyan Board (Social Welfare Board), organized Khadi-promotion activities (activities in support of India's home-spun cloth). She passed on her devotion for social activism to my mother.

Growing up at the height of India's freedom struggle, Gandhian ideals of truth and non-violence were inspiring the whole country, and the world beyond, earning Gandhi the title of "Mahatma" (the great one). My grandparents raised my parents to become firm believers in those ideals, imparting in my parents a sense of pride to have been born in families that upheld those values at that time.

With Gandhian ideals came dedication to service and regard for the poor. My grandfathers were both lawyers, supporting the needs of the poor, weak and downtrodden people of India, at the height of India's freedom movement against British rule. With these values in mind, my paternal grandparents established "*Sarvahitkarini Sabha*" –a Society devoted to service for the good of all. On a recent visit to Rajgarh, it was heartwarming to see how this society is still active today and continues to serve the needs of the poor.

Living a life-style free of greed and arrogance, the pursuit of vegetarianism and the respect for life in all forms, with the unshakeable belief in love and support of the family have been hallmarks of my parents' life. It was customary for a stream of visitors to come to my maternal grandparents' home, even at odd hours of day and night. No visitor was ever turned away; in fact they were welcomed with warm smiles, food, and an open heart. In particular, my grandparents welcomed the so-called 'untouchables', with the desire to teach by example at a time when social divisions and prejudice were rampant and exploited in India by those in power. My mother acquired from this, an endearing and welcoming attitude and social skills, and a conviction that allows her to open her heart and home to people of all background, always welcoming them with a warm smile and plenty of food.

Finally, my parents are believers in the plant-based diet. Anu-Gita in the Mahabharata is the oldest scripture in the world to explicitly recommend such a diet, based on the teaching of respect and humility towards the value of all life on earth. A plant-based diet is also complemented by the principles of non-violence and peace, and is recognized for being instrumental for good health and a spiritual mind, body and soul. As life long vegetarians, my parents have helped us to understand the value of a vegetarian or vegan diet, and my mother's recipes have taught us new ways to cook and enjoy a plant-based diet for healthy and peaceful living.

Devotion to hard work in the service of others, and a profound love of their children and grandchildren – these are the central qualities of my parents. We love them so much and I close this foreword with the hope that readers will find this compilation inspirational.

I dedicate this book to my parents Satya and Urmila, for teaching us life's purpose.

—SEEMA AGARWAL-HARDING

PREFACE

The expression *'Practical Vedanta'* was coined by Swami Vivekananda in 1896. He delivered several lectures in London and explained how Bhagavad - Gita has stressed the need to adjust religious practices to changes in time, place and circumstances. What is needed now, he said, is to update Traditional Vedanta. How it will make Vedanta "Practical" - this was outlined by him in the following words:

> *"Shankaracharya arose and revived the Vedanta philosophy. He worked out, rationalized, and placed before men the wonderful coherent system of Advaita. This was accomplished more than a thousand years ago. Today I feel that the practical aspect of Vedanta should be emphasized. For this purpose, along with the Upanishads, teachings of Buddha will have to be used...In Buddha, we had the great, universal heart and infinite patience, making religion more practical and bringing it to everyone's door. In Shankaracharya, we saw tremendous intellectual power, throwing the scorching light of reason upon everything. We want today the bright sun of intellectuality, joined with the heart of Buddha, the wonderful infinite heart of love and mercy. This union will give us the highest philosophy. Science and religion will meet and shake hands. Poetry and philosophy will become friends. This will be the religion of the future... ."*

After returning to Calcutta, Vivekananda called a meeting of monks and lay devotees on 1st May 1897. He told them about his desire to form an organization, which would try to improve the miserable social conditions. After allowing adequate time for consideration, a follow-up meeting was held on 5th May 1897. At that meeting, Ramakrishna Mission was formally established as a non-political organization, with the motto "*atmano moksartham jagad – hitaya ca*" (working, not only for one's own good, but also for the good of the world).

Thus Vivekananda made "*jagad–hitam*" (good of the world) an integral part of Practical Vedanta. While Vedanta had glorified "*moksa*" (individual salvation), Practical Vedanta emphasized "social welfare". Obviously, this signaled the start of the Spiritual Revolution of modern India, which won universal acclaim.

The concept of "*jagad–hitam*" (the good of the world), to be effective and meaningful, must include both spiritual and secular aspects, and in due course of time, the welfare of non-humans too. Furthermore, since Ramakrishna Mission was established as a non-political organization, the task of extending Practical Vedanta to the political field was a challenge to be met in the 20th Century.

Luckily for the world, Tilak–Aurobindo–Tagore–Gandhi took Practical Vedanta to great heights in the 20th Century. "*Jagad–hitam*" was their motto too, and they struggled and won the political independence of India, using the Gita as their manifesto. At this point, just a glimpse of these four contributions needs to be given.

Two of the most important contributions of Tilak were: (a) He wrote "Gita-Rahasya or Karmayoga–Shastra" – a detailed commentary on the Gita, which has been recognized as both scholarly and revolutionary; and (b) He revolutionized the political ideology of the Indian National Congress, and he was the first political prisoner in 1897.

Aurobindo supported Tilak in the freedom struggle till 1910, when he went to Pondicherry. There he wrote his famous Gita commentary entitled "Essays on the Gita". Among the many outstanding features of this book, the one which is particularly relevant for our purpose, was his scholarly opinion against the "*jagad – mithya*" doctrine of Traditional Vedanta. Earlier, the promotion of "*jagad – hitam*" had implicitly rejected "*jagad – mithya*".

Tagore's "*Gitanjali*", after the award of the Nobel Prize for Literature in 1913, helped spread Vedantic messages all over the world. The message of one-ness of all beings was beautifully conveyed through hymn no. 63:-

"When one knows Thee
Then alien there is none,
Then no door is shut.
Oh, grant me my prayer
That I may never lose
The bliss of the touch of the one
in the play of the many."

Through Hymn No. 10, he tried to arouse sympathy towards the poorest members of the society:-

"Pride can never approach
to where Thou keepest company
with the companionless
among the poorest, the lowliest, and the lost."

Tagore's "*Shanti-Niketan*", and worldwide travels for the cause of peace-oriented education was widely appreciated as the poet's strong appeal for world peace during the first forty years of the 20th Century (i.e. before the establishment of the United Nations). "Tagore's deepest regret, when he approached the date of his death in 1941," writes Uma Das Gupta, "was that his work of village reconstruction could not remove social injustice. He put his absolute faith in Gandhi's leadership to help the destitute millions."

Gandhi became the world-recognized champion of the Vedantic message of Ahimsa, to which he gave a path-breaking socio-political role. His successful campaign for the cause of human rights in South Africa during 1906-1914, earned him honor as "Mahatma". Through his non-violent confrontation with the British authorities in India, he encouraged women also to play a significant role—thus promoting the cause of women's empowerment. He risked his life, while attempting to remove the centuries-old curse of untouchability. He also promoted vegetarianism.

In the beginning of the 21st century, Western scholars and activists (drawing inspiration from Vedanta and other philosophies) have taken the lead in further updating of Vedanta, by attaching high priority to the welfare of non-humans. This has been done by means of "veganism", which is non-dairy vegetarianism. With the publication of the book "The World Peace Diet" in 2005, Will Tuttle's bold initiative has acquired the effectiveness of a revolutionary campaign. Through his work, Tuttle is contributing to global efforts in the cause of climate change and world peace.

This book is divided into two parts. Part I is entitled, "Spiritual Revolution for the Good of the World." It contains six chapters, describing the work of various Vedantins who have inspired my parents. This is a big subject and many Vedantins have made (and are still making) significant contributions. Chapter 6 of Part I marks the beginning of an effort by a 21st Century Vedantin, Will Tuttle, who is focusing on the issue of a vegan diet for a more compassionate and peaceful world.

Part II is a presentation on Practical Vedanta through poetic reflections written originally in Hindi by Urmila Agarwal, their English meaning drafted by Seema Agarwal-Harding and subsequently the reflections and their meaning given shape by both the authors – my parents. For the convenience of readers, the Hindi version is accompanied with its simplified meaning in English (not a strict translation).

ACKNOWLEDGEMENT

Our special thanks go to Dr. Tuttle who accepted our request and provided one chapter.

The drafting of the rest of this book was a family project. When the draft was being finalized, valuable feedback came informally from close friends, and through various family occasions in which the poetic reflections were shared. Amongst the close friends included Dr. Bhu Dev Sharma, Shri Gulab Khandelwal, Shri Himendra Thakur, Dr. M.M. Goel, Dr. Sham Narula, Dr. Rajan Narayanan, Dr. Satish Misra, Dr. R.S. Dwivedi, Dr. Anil and Babli Chopra, Dr. Sushil and Pratibha Sharma, Dr. Ashok and Mukta Shukla, Dr. Pooran and Kusum Shukla, Dr. Dinesh Sinha, Dr. Ramesh and Seema Godbole, Dr. Narendra and Chand Arora, Sharan Prasad, Santosh Aggarwal, Jaishriben, Anju Khanna, and Ila Desai.

Technical and moral support came from all the members of the family, Nishkam and Kokila, David, grandchildren Isha, Kiran, Priya and Maya, and more recently, son-in-law, James. Close relatives who rendered valuable help include Abhay Bhushan and Cybelle, Vinod Kashyap, Madan Mohan and Shashi Agarwal, Prabhat and Ambika Agarwal, Arun and Ritu Gupta, Veena and Anil Kumar, Manju and Dhanendra Kumar, Renu Mital, Dr. K.M. Mital, Rakesh and Alka Mital, Ruchi and Janmejay, Anil Narang, Savita and Anil Agarwal, Mrs. N.S. Choudhury. To all, and many more, too many to mention here, we express our sincere thanks and remain grateful for their love and support to us in helping complete this project.

Readers' suggestions and reactions are welcome, which will be incorporated into the next edition.

Columbia, Maryland
15 April, 2017

SATYA P. AGARWAL
URMILA AGARWAL
Email: ishamaya@rcn.com

Editor - SEEMA AGARWAL-HARDING
Email: seema.agarwalharding@gmail.com

Contents

PART I

Spiritual Revolution for the Good of the World

PART I

Spiritual Revolution for the Good of the World

Introduction

1.0.1 Romain Rolland has drawn special attention to the fact that Naren (i.e. the future Vivekananda), during his college days (1881), "was fired by the French Revolution." In continuation, we want to point out that Vivekananda himself started in 1896, the Spiritual Revolution. We are happy that the whole world knows about the French Revolution. The purpose of writing this book is to speed up the process of making the Spiritual Revolution known to more and more people, particularly because it started integrating the ancient philosophy of Vedanta with the noblest cause, viz. "Good of the World."

1.0.2 A unique feature of the spiritual Revolution is that, although it was non-political to start with, its scope has since been amazingly widened, and thinkers and activists from many countries have made, and are still making, big contributions. It is a fascinating and long story; here we present it briefly.

1.0.3 Part I has six chapters. Chapter 1.1 explains how Vivekananda's revolutionary vision was developed over about fifteen years, and announced publicly in London in 1896. He called it "Practical Vedanta", which symbolized beautifully his message that ancient teachings must be updated so as to ensure their relevance to the changing needs of the world. Vivekananda wanted traditional philosophers to understand that the modern society needed a harmonious combination of the spiritual and the secular, i.e. a warm handshake between religion and science. Obviously, such a revolutionary task represented a long-term effort to overcome orthodoxy and rigidity, and Vivekananda made it clear that the change would be brought about by dialogue and discussion, without any use of force. Vivekananda's open-minded approach enabled him to learn, not only from Buddha, but also from the West. Vivekananda established, in 1897, a new organization called "Ramakrishna Mission", and Chapter 1.1 narrates briefly how social welfare activities were carried out under very difficult circumstances.

1.0.4 Chapter 1.2 describes how Tilak used the Gita for India's freedom struggle, thus introducing the political dimension in Practical Vedanta. His scholarly book "*Gita – Rahasya*" is a revolutionary commentary, free from methodological errors from which Shankaracharya's treatise suffered.

1.0.5 Chapter 1.3 summarizes selectively Aurobindo's "Essays on the Gita" (written at Pondicherry), which rejected the "*jagat-mithya*" doctrine of Shankaracharya. Aurobindo had earlier been a strong supporter of Tilak.

1.0.6 Chapter 1.4 gives a brief account of Tagore's two big achievements:

(a) award of Nobel Prize for Literature to "*Gitanjali*"; and
(b) world-wide travels to promote the cause of world peace through peace-oriented education.

1.0.7 Chapter 1.5 outlines Gandhi's multi-dimensional contributions. Gandhi strengthened the Practical Vedanta Movement by his marvelous formulation of Ahimsa-based technique of social action, which he called "*Satyagraha*". His pioneering use of "*Satyagraha*" for the cause of human rights in South Africa, and finally his Rishi-like struggle for India's freedom from British-rule, are so well-known that we do not consider it necessary to write in detail.

1.0.8 Chapter 1.6 provides the writing of Will Tuttle from an earlier work entitled "Circles of Compassion" under the title *Unrecognized roots of injustice and the Vegan transformation.* With permission from Tuttle, the authors have included the chapter with a new heading "Meeting the challenges of the 21st Century", in an effort to highlight the central importance of veganism for cultivating a more compassionate world, in line with the principles of Practical Vedanta.

This is a big subject, and the authors introduce this concept in this compilation, to mark the beginning of their new writings, which will be developed in subsequent publications.

CHAPTER 1.1

Revolutionary Vision of Vivekananda and Activities of Ramakrishna Mission

1.1.1 Vivekananda's desire to improve social conditions has been traced by Romain Rolland to his college days. After graduation, he became a disciple of Sri Ramakrishna, and among other things, he learnt the importance of doing "*sewa*" (service) of the poor, seeing God in them. This was the second stage of his spiritual journey, which Vivekananda himself considered the most important. The third stage was, his walking on foot, all over India, culminating in the Kanyakumari Resolve. Finally, it was towards the end of his three-year-long stay in the West, that he made a public announcement in London. He coined the expression "Practical Vedanta".

1.1.2 Thus the development and manifestation of Vivekananda's revolutionary vision took about fifteen years, and there were four significant stages:

(a) Education at Calcutta University
(b) Training by Sri Ramakrishna
(c) Walking on foot, all over India, culminating in the Kanyakumari Resolve
(d) Contact with Western scholars

A brief look at each of these stages makes it clear why Vivekananda decided to strike at the root of the problem, *viz. how to modify* Vedanta so as to give priority to social welfare activities.

Education at Calcutta University

1.1.3 During his college days, Vivekananda was Narendra Nath Datta or Naren for short (that was his pre-monkhood name). From his boyhood, Naren exhibited talents in several fields and the rich family circumstances enabled him to cultivate as many of them as he could possibly do. Romain Rolland has described how broad-based was his university education:

> "At college, he was distinguished for his brilliant intellect, embracing with equal zest the sciences, astronomy, mathematics, philosophy, and Indian as well as foreign languages. He read the English and Sanskrit poets. He devoured the historical works of Green and Gibbon. He was fired by the French Revolution..."[1]

1.1.4 Reading about revolutionary changes in Europe caused a stir in Naren's mind, and he wondered if a day would come when Indians too would shout – Liberty, Equality, Fraternity.

Training by Sri Ramakrishna

1.1.5 Sri Ramakrishna had the ability to recognize the great potential and leadership qualities of Naren, and he gradually prepared him to be the head of the group of sincere devotees who would carry out the Master's Mission after he himself passed away. He never concealed his feelings about Naren's future destiny. When Naren implored the Master to show him the way to "*nirvikalpa samadhi*" - the attainment of final bliss after surrendering all earthly ties- he was administered a sharp rebuke from Sri Ramakrishna: "Fie on you! I never thought you so mean as to be anxious for your own salvation only, whereas you have powers to do much good to mankind."

At Vivekanada's insistent request, the Master one day gave him a glimpse of it and said, "Just as a treasure is locked up in a box, so the realization of the supreme bliss will be locked up and the key shall remain with me. You have work to do."[2]

1.1.6 Sri Ramakrishna also taught Naren that the proper way of doing good to mankind was to view it as worship to God, and that it was sheer arrogance if any feeling of superiority were to be associated with compassion. As the Master put it –

> "Compassion! Who are you to be compassionate? God alone can have compassion for the mortal. But service to man should be done as worship to God – *Jiva* is none else than *Siva.*" Naren understood what the Master had in mind, and he told his friends, "Today I have heard a new Truth of great significance. In time I shall broadcast this for humanity."[3]

1.1.7 A mysterious incident symbolizing the transmittal of special powers from Sri Ramakrishna to Naren, as confirmed by Vivekananda himself, has been described by Majumdar as follows: "Knowing that his end was imminent, the Master, in order to endow Naren with the spiritual wealth which he himself had acquired after years of superhuman efforts and unprecedented austerities, called him to his side, only three or four days before his *mahasmadhi.* Having seated him in front and looking intently into the eyes of his dear disciple, he fell into a deep trance. Naren felt the powerful impact of a tremendous force entering into his own body and soon lost all body consciousness. When, after a while, Naren came to himself, the Master was found shedding tears. When interrogated, Sri Ramakrishna softly replied, "Oh Naren, today I have given you my all and have become a *fakir* (beggar). By the force of the power transmitted by me, great things will be done by you, and only after that, will you go to whence you came."[4]

1.1.8 Naren also learnt from the Master the supreme lesson that it is more "glorious to help even one man" than to be freed from the cycle of birth and death. In the pre-Ramakrishna Hindu tradition as commonly understood (or rather, misunderstood), personal salvation or *Mukti* was viewed as the highest attainment, and taking birth in the *samsara* (for whatever reason) was considered a symbol of imperfection. Sri Ramakrishna, by his own example, helped revive the social service-oriented Hindu view, which was close to the Bodhisattva ideal of putting the salvation of all above one's own salvation. In the closing days of his worldly life, Sri Ramakrishna permitted visitors to seek his guidance on spiritual matters, even though doctors wanted him to take complete rest. As Romain Rolland put it – He never turned anybody away. He said, "Let me be condemned to be born over and over again, even in the form of a dog, if so I can be of help to a single soul!"

And again, "I will give up twenty thousand such bodies to help one man. It is glorious to help even one man!"

He even reproached himself for his ecstasies, because they took time that might otherwise have been given to others: "O Mother, stop me from enjoying them! Let me stay in my normal state, so that I can be of more use in the world."

During his last days when his disciples protected him in spite of himself from the importunity of devotees, he said, "How I suffer because no one needs any help today!"[5]

Walking on Foot All over India, Culminating in the Kanyakumari Resolve

1.1.9 Romain Rolland has pointed out the uniqueness of these walks:

> "He wandered, free from plan, caste, home, constantly alone with God. And there was no single hour of his life when he was not brought into contact with the sorrows, the desires, the abuses, the misery, and the feverishness of living men, rich and poor, in town and field; he became one with their lives; the great Book of Life revealed to him what all the books in the libraries could not have done (for after all they are only collections), which even Ramakrishna's ardent love had only been able to see dimly as in a dream –

the tragic face of the present day, the God struggling in humanity, the cry of the peoples of India." [6]

1.1.10 What bothered Vivekananda even more than the poverty itself, was the gulf between the rich and the poor, between the strong and the weak, and further, the ugly sight of the strong dealing a death-blow to those who are comparatively weak, without any standard of morality. "Is this a country or hell?" he asked, "a country where millions of people live on the flower of the *Mohua* plant, and a million or two of *sadhus*, and a hundred million or so of *Brahmins* suck the blood of these poor people, without even the least effort for their amelioration? This is our native land, he bemoaned, where huts and palaces existed side-by-side."

"Worn-out huts by the very side of palaces, piles of refuse in the near proximity of temples, the *samnyasin* clad only with a little loin-cloth, walking by the gorgeously dressed, the pitiful gaze of lusterless eyes of the hunger-stricken at the well-fed and the amply-provided." [7]

1.1.11 With such a wide gulf between the rich and the poor, asked Vivekanada, how can we have unity and fellow-feeling which are the secrets of national greatness? Born, as it were, a disunited mob, we cannot combine. All these dissentions pained Vivekananda and he remarked:

> "If one of our countrymen stands up and tries to become great, we all try to hold him down, but if a foreigner comes and tries to kick us, it is all right. We have been used to such slavery, have we not?"..."We are intensely selfish. Not three of us can come together without hating each other, without being jealous of each other. Why should the Hindu nation with all its wonderful intelligence and other things have gone to pieces? I would answer you, Jealousy. Because of this, we also lack organization and coordination of wills..."[8]

1.1.12 Oppression of the masses, according to Vivekanada, was a big factor leading to the downfall of the country.

Another equally significant factor was tyranny over women. The way they were kept under conditions of servile dependence on men made them so weak as to be "good only to weep at the slightest approach of a mishap or danger."[9]

Evil customs were particularly injurious to women – viz. child marriage, big gap in the ages of husbands and wives, ill treatment of widows, and so on. What pained Vivekananda was that evil customs were being adhered to in the name of religion. "A girl of eight is married to a man of thirty and the parents are jubilant over it. And if any one protests against it, the plea is put forward, our religion is being overturned."[10]

1.1.13 Of the many angles from which the social problems of India could be analyzed – economic, political, sociological, historical, cultural, religious and spiritual – Vivekananda placed the greatest emphasis on the religious and spiritual. He based this on his interpretation of what has been the "nerve-center" of India's life from time immemorial:

> "We made our choice ages ago, and we must abide by it...Each nation, like each individual, has one theme in this life, which is its center, the principal note around which every other note comes to form the harmony. In India, religious life forms the center, the keynote of the whole music of national life...Social reform in India has to be preached by showing how much more spiritual a life the new system will bring; and politics has to be preached by showing how much it will improve the one thing that the nation wants – its spirituality."[11]

1.1.14 The linkage between religion and social conditions has to be understood as explaining both the positive and the negative aspects, in the sense that, while social progress in the past rested on religious maturity, a deterioration in the social situation at present could be traced back to religious perversion. The root cause of India's downfall was the unwillingness of religious leaders to give up orthodoxy and to make adjustments in religious practices in tune with the changing needs of the society. Vivekananda linked India's doom to ritual-centered priest-craft, rigidity of outlook, superstitions, and refusal to learn the good points of Buddhism.

The last point in this list (viz. lack of mutual understanding between Hindus and Buddhists) was responsible for the easy victory of foreign invaders in Sind—a warning for the catastrophic downfall of India that occurred later, to which, unfortunately, the religious leaders of those days paid no serious attention.

1.1.15 "Having forgotten the true spirit of religion as well as the social-welfare aspect of Vedantic philosophy", said Vivekananda, "the priestly class made fools of common people by pushing them blindly from one ritual to another, from one evil custom to another. Caste distinctions became more and more rigid, and those who did the most difficult and the most important job of keeping the country clean, were pushed down and declared untouchables. Religious and philosophical orthodoxy supported compartmentalization and untouchability, and encouraged those who lay down hard and fast rules as to who can marry whom and who can dine with whom. People discussed for years such meaningless questions as whether to take food with the right hand or the left. "If such a country does not go to ruin, what else will?" asked Vivekananda. He wanted the philosophers to broaden their outlook, and appealed to the perpetrators of social tyranny to "come out of your narrow holes."

> "Hide your faces in shame. A race of dotards, you lose your caste if you come out. Sitting down those hundreds of years with an ever-increasing load of crystallized superstition on your heads, spending all your energy upon discussing the touchableness or untouchableness of this food or that person, with all humanity crushed out of you by the continuous social tyranny of ages – What are you? And what are you doing now? ... Kick out old ideas that have ruined the

country. Come out of your narrow holes, and look forward!"[12]

1.1.16 Vivekanada's walks and reflections culminated in what is commonly called "The Kanyakumari Resolve", about which he himself wrote in a letter from America:

> "At Cape Comorin, sitting in Mother Kumari's temple, sitting on the last bit of Indian rock, I hit upon a plan. We are so many *samnyasins* wandering about and teaching the people metaphysics – it is all madness. Did not our Gurudeva say: *An empty stomach is no good for religion?* That these poor people are leading a life of brutes is simply due to lack of right knowledge. Suppose some disinterested *samnyasins*, bent on doing good to others and on effectively lessening their misery, go from village to village, disseminating practical knowledge and seeking in various ways to better the condition of all down to the *chandala*, through oral teaching and by means of maps, cameras, globes and such other accessories – can't that bring forth good in time? ...We, as a nation, have lost our individuality, and that is the cause of all mischief in India. We have to give back to the nation its lost individuality and raise the masses. We have to make Vedanta social-welfare-oriented."[13]

1.1.17 Subsequently, it became clear to Vivekanada why the poor villagers were not looked after by *Vedantins*. Based on Chapter 4 of the Gita, they had interpreted *Vedantic* knowledge as "Identity of Atman and Brahman". So they thought of devoting all their energy to attaining their own moksha, and felt that they had no responsibility to worry about the miserable living conditions of the poor. Vivekananda would change the situation by reminding the *Vedantins* that Chapter 13 of the Gita defined knowledge as "one-ness of all beings". The Vedantic prayer is "*sarve bhavantu sukhinah*" (i.e. may all be happy). So Vivekananda would make the *Vedantins* realize that it is their responsibility to improve living conditions of the poor.

Contact with Western Scholars

1.1.18 Vivekananda's participation in the Parliament of World Religions in 1893 brought him into close contact with Western scholars (who were themselves concerned with the problem of modernization of religious ideas in their own society). After the Parliament, he was invited to stay in USA. He gave lectures at various organizations. These lectures (in USA and Europe) were spread over more than three years, and gave him an excellent opportunity, not only to present Indian ideas, but also to listen to the views of Western scholars. They told him (among other things), that, living under the political and administrative control of British officials (whose main responsibility was maintenance of law and order), Indians had mostly seen the "negative side" of Europe. But Europe also had an impressive "positive side". It was in Europe and America that people struggled to make revolutionary changes in the social set-up. Advancement of the scientific spirit went hand-in-hand with changes in the religious outlook. In fact, revolution in thought had preceded revolution on the streets. Women came out of their households and made a very valuable contribution to improve the quality of the nation's life and to bring about all-round development. Revolutionary ideas were spread among people by means of effective organizational skills.

1.1.19 It was in London that Vivekananda finally made a public announcement is 1896 of his decision to update Traditional Vedanta and to call it "Practical Vedanta". In his own words:

> "We want today the bright sun of Shankaracharya's intellectuality, joined with the heart of Buddha, the wonderful infinite heart of love and mercy. This union will give us the highest philosophy. Science and religion will meet and shake hands. Poetry and philosophy will become friends. This will be the religion of the future."[14]

Establishment of Ramakrishna Mission

1.1.20 After returning to Calcutta, Vivekananda called a meeting of monks and lay devotees on 1st May 1897. He was convinced, he said, that lack of proper organization was a serious defect in Hindu society. Traditional "*sampradayas*" were rather self-centered and usually had a narrow, sectarian outlook. Buddhists had a comparatively broader vision, and they established contacts with more and more people. Vivekanada appealed for cooperation of all in order to organize successfully, educational, health, and other service activities.

1.1.21 At a follow-up meeting on 5th May 1897, Ramakrishna Mission was formally established, as a non-political organization, with the motto "*atmano moksartham jagad-hitaya ca*", i.e. working not only for one's own good, but for the good of the world. "The aim of the Mission is to preach those truths which Sri Ramakrishna has, for the good of humanity, preached and demonstrated by practical application in his own life, and to help others to put these truths into practice in their lives, for their temporal, mental and spiritual advancement."[15]

Exemplary Dedication and Widening Coverage of Service Activities

1.1.22 From the start, Vivekananda was confident of a successful fulfillment of his vision. His optimism was expressed in letters that he wrote to his friends. For example, his letter to Mary Hale dated July 1897 ran like this – "Only one idea was burning in my brain – to start the machine for elevating the Indian masses, and that I have succeeded in doing to a certain extent. It would have made your heart glad to see how my boys are working in the midst of famine and disease and misery – nursing by the mat-bed of the cholera-stricken pariah and feeding the starving *chandala*, and the Lord sends help to me, to them, to all."[16]

1.1.23 Within one year, the new organization had to face an extremely serious public health problem. In April 1898, when Vivekananda was in Darjeeling to recoup his health, news reached him of the outbreak of plague in Calcutta. On 3rd May, he reached Calcutta. He saw people terrified by plague, and dismayed by the plague-regulations. It was as if a storm were about to burst over Calcutta. People were fleeing in panic. Troops were called in to quell the riots. Vivekananda at once grasped the gravity of the situation. He drafted a plague manifesto in Bengali as well as in Hindi. He announced that relief operations will be started immediately. When a brother-monk asked him, "Swamiji, where will the funds come from?" he replied with a sudden fierceness of decision, "Why, we shall sell the newly-bought *Matha*-grounds, if necessary! We are *samnyasins*; we must be ready to sleep under trees and live on daily *bhiksa*, as we did before. What! Should we care for *Matha* and possessions when by disposing of them we could relieve thousands suffering before our eyes![17] Fortunately, this extreme step was not necessary, for Vivekananda soon received promises of ample funds for his immediate work.

1.1.24 When plague again broke out in 1899, the Ramakrishna Mission undertook relief work under the leadership of Sadananda, assisted by Sister Nivedita and others. About Sister Nivedita's part in the work, we have it on the authority of the historian, Sir Jadunath Sarkar, an eyewitness: "When the sweepers had fled away, he chanced upon a white woman one day clearing the streets with broom and basket in hand. This was none other than Nivedita, whose courage and sense of civic duty spurred the local youth to take up the cleansing of the lanes and streets, following her example, and thus make their quarters free from the threat of the pestilence."[18]

1.1.25 Sadananda himself similarly set an unprecedented example. If the stench of garbage accumulated in a narrow lane repelled even the practiced sweepers, he would nonchalantly snatch the basket and spade from one of them and set about removing the decomposed heap till the sweepers too would step forward to help him. At the end, he would congratulate them and embrace them warmly, regardless of their social distance and dirty clothes. Or if there was an uncared-for patient, he would hug him and nurse him to recovery.

1.1.26 These examples bring out in bold relief the ideal of service enunciated by Vivekananda and the dedication of his close associates. Obviously, the new organization not only started strongly, but also had high quality human resources for maintaining the standard of service.

1.1.27 Almost 120 years have elapsed since the Ramakrishna Mission faced the initial challenges of rendering service to the needy under the most difficult circumstances. The fact that this institution has kept up the spirit of dedication, and simultaneously widened the coverage of service activities, is a tribute to Vivekananda and his followers. Although a detailed account of such developments would make this chapter too long, we mention briefly that the social service activities of the Ramakrishna Mission now cover as many as six broad areas:

(i) Educational work
(ii) Health work
(iii) Cultural activities
(iv) Rural uplift
(v) Tribal welfare
(vi) Youth movement.

1.1.28 Indira Patel, after describing the work being done by the Ramakrishna Mission in each field, singles out 'the inculcation of the right attitude', as a special feature of the Mission's training:

> "One point which should be made clear is that the Mission's centers enlist youths or disciples and train them as social workers, the only difference between the academic training and the training imparted in the *Matha* lies in the initial emphasis on discipline,

> both mental and physical, with a view to inculcating the right attitude over and above generating a sensitivity, so essential in all social work."[19]

1.1.29 Special mention should be made of Swami Ranganathananda's famous book entitled "Practical Vedanta and the Science of Values", published by Advaita Ashram, Calcutta, in 1995. This book is based on four lectures that Swamiji delivered in 1992. He referred to his correspondence with the eminent biologist Julian Huxley, and suggested that, for obtaining the cooperation of modern intellectuals, Practical Vedanta needs to be presented as a value-based movement. "Good-of-all" is the right value for the modern world.

Welfare of Non-Human Beings

1.1.30 In his first lecture on Practical Vedanta, delivered in London in 1896, Swami Vivekananda expressed the hope that, in due course of time, welfare of non-human beings will also receive proper attention:

> "The ideal is not to eat flesh, not to injure any being, for all animals are my brothers. If you can think of them as your brothers, you have made a little headway towards the brotherhood of all souls, which Vedanta teaches."[20]

1.1.31 Summary of Vivekananda's contribution to Practical Vedanta

(a) He coined the term "Practical Vedanta", and was the founder of the Practical Vedanta Movement.

(b) He introduced "*jagad-hitam*" as the distinguishing feature of Practical Vedanta. Implicitly, he rejected the "*jagad-mithya*" doctrine of Shankaracharya.

(c) His vision of "*jagad-hitam*" was comprehensive, and covered both spiritual and secular aspects. Among secular issues, he mentioned untouchability, poverty, education, and women's status in society.

(d) He coined the term *"Daridra-Narayan"* and appealed to the people to "serve the poor, seeing God in them." Because of his initiative, *"Sewa-yoga"* became the most popular synonym of *karmayoga.*

(e) He started the open-ended process of making Vedanta universal.

(f) He established Ramakrishna Mission and made sure that the work he had started was installed on permanent footing.

(g) His writings and speeches (which have been published) are a valuable addition to the world's inspirational literature.

Endnotes

[1] Romain Rolland, *The Life of Ramakrishna,* Advaita Ashram, Calcutta, Eighth edition, 1970, pp. 223-4

[2] R.C. Majumdar, *Swami Vivekananda: An Historical Review.* General Printers, Calcutta, 1915, pp. 19-20

[3] Indira Patel, *Vivekananda's Approach to Social Work,* Sri Ramakrishna Math, Madras, 1987, p.1

[4] R.C. Majumdar, *Swami Vivekananda: An Historical Review, op. cit.,* pp. 20-1

[5] Romain Rolland, *The Life of Ramakrishna, op. cit.,* pp. 258-9

[6] Romain Rolland, *The Life of Vivekananda* and *The Universal Gospel,* Advaita Ashram, Calcutta, 1970, p.21

[7] *Swami Vivekananda, Complete Works* (eight volumes). Advaita Ashram, Calcutta, Fourteenth edition, 1972, Vol. V, p. 441

[8] R.C. Majumdar, *Swami Vivekananda: An Historical Review, op. cit.* p.121

[9] *Ibid.,* p.132

[10] *Ibid.,* p.132

[11] *Swami Vivekananda, Complete Works, op. cit.,* Vol. III, pp. 220-2

[12] *Ibid.,* Vol. V, p.10

[13] D.S. Sarma, *The Renaissance of Hinduism.* Banaras Hindu University, 1944, p. 265

[14] *Swami Vivekananda, Complete Works, op. cit.,* Vol. II, p.140

[15] R.C. Majumdar, *Swami Vivekananda: An Historical Review, op. cit.,* pp. 69-70

[16] *Ibid.,* p.111

[17] *Life of Swami Vivekananda by his Eastern and Western Disciples.* Advaita Ashram, Calcutta, Fifth edition, 1981, Vol. II, p. 328

[18] R.C. Majumdar, *Swami Vivekananda: An Historical Review, op. cit.,* p 72

[19] Indira Patel, *Vivekananda's Approach to Social Work, op. cit.,* p.92

[20] *Swami Vivekananda, Complete Works, op. cit.,* Vol. II

CHAPTER 1.2

Tilak's Revolutionary Interpretation of the Gita

1.2.1 Tilak is known as the most revolutionary political leader of India for 25 years (1893-1918), and also the internationally famous author of "*Gita Rahasya*", which he wrote in Mandalay jail in Marathi. People of India expressed their admiration by calling him "*Lokmanya*" (revered by the people). For purposes of the present book, we briefly narrate how he strengthened the Practical Vedanta Movement.

Revolutionary Orientation of the Indian National Congress

1.2.2 At a time when the Indian National Congress did not even dream of political independence, Tilak declared: "Without the power to shape our own destiny, our national regeneration in a larger sense cannot be effected. Don't think I am talking in the air – Bhagavad Gita will show us the way."[1]

A Significant Extension of Practical Vedanta

1.2.3 Tilak's use of the Gita for the freedom struggle widened the scope of Practical Vedanta. Prior to that, activities of Ramakrishna Mission founded by Vivekananda, were strictly non-political. The Indian National Congress was supposed to be a political party, but it only "made petitions". Tilak revolutionized the Congress Party's approach and made it fit for a fight against foreign rulers. For this, the British administration put him in jail. Thus Tilak was the first political prisoner.

Gita as the Manifesto of the Freedom Struggle

1.2.4 As a Practical Vedantin, Tilak viewed the hard life of a prisoner (in the company of criminals of all sorts), as *Tapas*, i.e. suffering for a social cause. This definition of *Tapas* was radically different from that given in Traditional Vedantic texts.

1.2.5 Not only Tapas, but several other words were interpreted by him in a new way, so as to make Gita a manifesto of the freedom struggle. For example, the first word of the Gita, viz. "*dharmaksetra*" was given a revolutionary meaning as pointed out by Thomas:

> "Tilak was the first Indian national leader to bring out the meaning of the righteous war (*dharmayuddha*), in the *dharmaksetra*, for modern India. He boldly stated that not only one's immediate field of activity but the whole of India is the *dharmaksetra* of modern India."[2]

1.2.6 Panikkar not only refers to Tilak's wider interpretation of *dharmaksetra*, but also finds a parallel between Arjuna's spirit of unmanliness at Kuruksetra and the inactivity which gripped the Indian society when Tilak was writing Gita-Rahasya:

> "To Tilak, India was the *dharmaksetra* – the field of righteousness – and the inactivity which seemed to have gripped India was but a reflection of the unmanliness that Arjuna felt on the field of battle. The Gita helped Arjuna to get rid of his dejection. The same purpose it can now fulfill on this new field of righteousness. To Tilak it was clear that it was only through the message of the Gita that India could save herself."[3]

1.2.7 Prior to Tilak, either *jnanayoga* or *bhaktiyoga* was given priority. Tilak explained that earlier commentators had committed methodological errors. We summarize Tilak's views in the following paragraphs.

Methodological Errors of Earlier Commentators

1.2.8 Tilak's views on methodology were explained by means of an ancient Sanskrit shloka, an English summary of which is provided in Radhakrishnan's words:

> "In determining the purpose of any treatise, we must see the question with which it opens (*upkrama*) and the conclusion to which it leads (*upasamhara*). The Gita opens with the following problem.Arjuna refuses to fight and raises difficulties. He puts up a plausible plea for absenteeism from activity and for retreat from the world, an ideal which dominated certain sects at the time of the composition of the Gita. To convert him is the purpose of the Gita. It raises the question whether action or renunciation of action is better and concludes that action is better. In the end, Arjuna declares that his perplexities are ended and he would carry out the command to fight. Right through, the teacher emphasizes the need for action. He does not adopt the solution of dismissing the world as an illusion and action as a snare. He recommends the full active life of man in the world with the inner life anchored in the Eternal Spirit. The Gita is therefore a mandate for action."[4]

Ancient commentators had not followed the above-mentioned approach.

Tilak also explained how Shankaracharya had used the method of "Arthavada" in an incorrect manner.

Making use of the Isha Upanishad, Shanti-Parva and Anu-Gita

1.2.9 Again, we quote a summary of Tilak's views, in Radhakrishnan's words:

(a) "If there is hostility to the method of works, it is not hostility to work as such but the theory of salvation by works. In popular language, this objection is expressed by saying that '*Karma* causes *Bandhan*'. But Isha Upanishad rejects this objection..."

(b) "Shankaracharya's statement, that *jnana* and *karma* can not go together, is rejected by *Shanti-Parva shlokas* 12.237.1 and 12.234.29."

(c) "Shankracharya's doctrine of *Karma-samnyasa* is rejected by *Shanti-Parva shlokas* 12.347.80-81."

(d) "Anu-Gita gives priority to Karma-yoga. It also elaborates Bhagavad-Gita *shloka* 3.20, which says that *Janaka* attained salvation by *Karmayoga,* through which he performed *Lokasamgraha,* that is, 'good of all'."[5]

Lokasamgraha (Good-of-All)

1.2.10 Tilak explains in detail that the teaching on *Lokasamgraha* is a special feature of the Gita, which goes beyond the teaching of the Upanishads. In Panikkar's words:

> "*Lokasamgraha* or the welfare of the world as the motive and object of all action is the special contribution of the Gita in Hindu religious and social thought. It follows naturally from the doctrine of unattached action, which is the central theme of Krishna's teaching. If action is to be selfless and is to be without reference to the fruits thereof (in relation to the actor) then the question naturally arises, why should anyone persist in a course of action? The old theories of *yajna* or sacrifice provided a simple answer: action is to please the gods and derive worldly benefits through them. Since this was not *Nishkama karma* or action without reference to the results for the actor, the Gita rejected it and supplied the answer that the object of all action should be Lokasamgraha or welfare of the world..."
>
> "The social theory behind *Lokasamgraha* doctrine of the Gita is most important. The conception of a world order, which it is the duty of the individual to uphold by dedicating his activity towards that end, runs all through the teachings of the Gita. The earlier Vedic religion had no such conception. Nor did the later

thinkers who built up the comprehensive structure of Upanishadic thought devote any attention to social development. For the first time the Gita gives a social content to religion and emphasizes the welfare of the world as the purpose of all action. The doctrine of sacrifice is thus given a wholly different meaning in the Gita, where action dedicated to God is called *Brahmayajna*."[6]

Comparison with Western Activism

1.2.11 Tilak's elaboration of *Lokasamgraha* was intended to show to the social reform-oriented, educated Indians that their attempts at copying the west arose only because they had not understood their own scriptures properly. In the nineteenth century, the reformist thinkers were, to begin with, impressed by the social purpose and wide humanism of Christianity, and the earliest stirrings of educated India were towards a dilution of Hindu religion with Christian thought, which was best exemplified by one of the phases of the *Brahmo-samaj*. Brown explains why, in Tilak's opinion, the *Lokasamgraha* approach was better suited to India than the social action philosophy borrowed from the West:

> "Tilak rejects the activism of the West adopted by his Brahmin rival Gokhale, who believed in gradual social reform as a precedent to *Swaraj* or Indian independence. The *Lokasamgraha* insisted on the ousting of the British and upon self-rule as a pre-requisite to all else. He characterized Western-type activism as devoted merely to improving worldly existence, whereas the *Karmayoga* of the Gita was devoted to self-realization through service to mankind. The Western energism was thus '*rajasi*' or emotional while the Indian variety was *sattvika* or intelligent."[7]

Viewing Householders as Pillars of Social Action

1.2.12 Tilak himself broadly accepted the metaphysical concept of the *Advaita* philosophy of Shankaracharya whom he called "a superman and a great sage". But the Gita-commentary of Tilak, being *karmayoga*-oriented, was drastically different from the *jnana*-centered commentary of Shankaracharya. Furthermore, as part of his argument establishing the inadequacy of "*jnana-without-karma*", Tilak also criticized Shankaracharya for removing the prohibition on *samnyasa* or renunciation, Tilak quoted Smriti texts to assert that, in the *kaliyuga*, that is, after the days of the *Kauravas* and the *Pandavas*, the path of renunciation was prohibited. In fact, five things were forbidden: cow slaughter; meat eating at the *shraddha* ceremonies in honor of ancestors; *Agnihotra* or maintenance of the perpetual sacred fire; *niyoga* or begetting offspring from another's wife; and *samnyasa*. Of these, Shankaracharya retained the first four prohibitions, but removed that on *samnyasa*, which according to Tilak, was partly responsible for a lukewarm attitude to the philosophy of activism as taught by the Gita. In Tilak's approach, the main responsibility for *Lokasamgraha* activities has to be borne by householders, not *samnyasins*.

1.2.13 Tilak's contention was that, not only in *Kaliyuga* but even prior to that, warnings were given about the disadvantages likely to be caused to the society by a widespread recourse to *samnyasa*. The practice of renunciation was encouraged by Buddhists and the Jains. In the *Bhagavad-Gita*, only an attitude of renunciation concerning the fruit of action is recommended, not renunciation of worldly duties as such. This Gita way of harmonizing the two ancient doctrines – *pravritti or karma*, and *nivritti or renunciation* – was, in Tilak's opinion, more beneficial to the society than that attempted by *Smriti* writers through the scheme of four *Ashramas*.

1.2.14 Smriti writers like Manu, devised the scheme of four *Ashramas*, out of which the second (*Grihastha*) would concentrate on *karma*, and the fourth (*samnyasa*) would concentrate on *jnana*. However, these writers had fully realized the fact that if there was an inordinate increase in the desire of the people to take up *samnyasa*, worldly activities would be adversely affected and society would ultimately be tamed. Therefore, Manu placed definite restrictions as to when *samnyasa ashram* could be entered into. In fact, he compared the *Grihastha Ashrama* to the sea, and the other three *Ashramas* to rivers (Manu 6.90). In as much as the state of the householder provides the other three states with food, Manu enjoined the performance of all worldly activities, including acts of valor and of universal welfare, during *Grihastha Ashrama*. He argued that in coming to birth, every man brings on his back three debts, which he owes to *Rishis*, his ancestors, and the *Vedic* deities. He must discharge these debts by fulfilling his obligations, namely, to the *Rishis* by the study of *Vedas*; to the ancestors by the procreation of offspring; and to the deities by the performance of spiritual ritual. If he takes to *samnyasa* without having discharged his obligations, he will go to perdition.

1.2.15 There are indications that in many cases, the preconditions for taking to *samnyasa* were not observed. Tilak refers to a story in the *Adiparva* of the *Mahabharata*, that *Jaratkaru* did not discharge his debt to the ancestors, and started austere religious practices preparatory for *samnyasa*, before marrying, and that as a result of his having thus destroyed the possibility of children, he saw his ancestors dangling in the air, and that, in performance of their injunctions he later married. Tilak also mentions another story that occurs in the *Bhagavata*. *Narada* advised the sons of *Daksa Prajapati* to take to the path of *samnyasa* before they had married. *Daksa Prajapati* reprimanded *Narada* for this unlawful and objectionable behavior, and laid a curse on him.

1.2.16 In later times, many instances of people taking to *samnyasa* as an easy way of escaping from worldly responsibilities must have occurred. *Tulsidas* in *Ramacharitmanas* refers to people who, after the death of their wife, and realizing that they were not able to maintain themselves as householders, shaved off their head and became *samnyasins*

(*Uttarkanda* 99.3). It was in anticipation of such occurrences that the *Smriti* – writers made *samnyasa* a *Kali-varjya,* that is prohibited in *Kaliyuga.* Tilak's *Gita-Rahasya* strongly supports such prohibition against *samnyasa,* which was however, removed by Shankaracharya.

Tilak's most Memorable Statements

1.2.17 Two statements made by Tilak in 1908 have become inextricably linked with his name in Indian history. As Sarma puts it:

> "Two of Tilak's utterances have justly become famous and are cherished by the nation. One is '*Swaraj* is my birthright and I will have it', and the other is his reply to the judge who convicted and transported him to Burma for six years in 1908: "Inspite of the verdict of the jury, I maintain I am innocent. There are higher powers that rule the destinies of things, and it may be the will of Providence that the cause which I represent should prosper more by my suffering than by my remaining free."[8]

Tilak Paved the Way for Gandhi

1.2.18 The years 1916-18 saw Tilak as the "uncrowned King of India", and even the Secretary of State, Mr. Montagu, wrote in his diary: "He (Tilak) is the politician who probably has the greatest influence of any person in India."

While Tilak was away in England, during most of 1919, the Gandhian era in India's freedom struggle began, and it was a significant coincidence that the first All-India Non-cooperation Movement under Gandhiji's leadership started on August 1st, 1920, just a few hours after Tilak had breathed his last. As Sarma puts it:

> "Doubtless, it is Tilak's mantle that has fallen on Mahatma Gandhi, and not that of Gokhale, though the Mahatma regards Gokhale as his political guru." [9]

1.2.19 Summary of Tilak's contribution to Practical Vedanta

(a) His use of the Gita for the freedom struggle was a contribution of historic importance.

(b) His monumental book "*Gita-Rahasya*" or "*Karma-Yoga-Shastra*" was a very valuable addition to Gita literature.

(c) He strengthened the Practical Vedanta Movement by pointing out that Shankaracharya's Gita-commentary suffers from serious methodological errors:

(i) Shankaracharya did not follow the standard method of interpretation based on "*upakarma-upasamhara-phala*" (reference para 1.2.8)

(ii) Shankaracharya used the method of "*arthavada*" (reference 1.2.8) in an incorrect manner

(iii) Shankaracharya started with a pre-determined conclusion, (favoring renunciation) and so had to twist the meaning of important *shlokas* to get that meaning.

Endnotes

1 T.V. Parvate, *Bal Gangadhar Tilak*, Navajivan, Ahmedabad, 1958, p. 477

2 P.M. Thomas, *Twentieth Century Indian Interpretations of Bhagavad – Gita:* Tilak, Gandhi and Aurobindo; Indian Society for promoting Christian Knowledge, Delhi, 1987, p.188

3 K.M. Panikkar, *The Foundations of New India*, Allen and Unwin, London, 1963, p.43

4 S. Radhakrishnan, *The Bhagavad-Gita.* Harper and Row, New York, 1973

5 *Ibid*

6 K.M. Panikkar, *The Foundations of New India, op. cit.*, pp. 39-40

7 D. Mackenzie Brown, *"The Philosophy of Bal Gangadhar Tilak: Karma* vs. *Jnana in Gita-Rahasya"*, in the Journal of Asian Studies, Vol. XVII, No. 2 (Feb. 1958), p. 202

8 D.S, Sarma, *The Renaissance of Hinduism*, Banaras Hindu University, 1944, p. 145

9 *Ibid*, p. 143

CHAPTER 1.3

Aurobindo's Rejection of the Jagat-Mithya Doctrine

1.3.1 Aurobindo's life (from the age of eight), had four distinct phases:

(a) Studying French, Greek, etc. in England (13 years);
(b) Teaching French, but making a self-study of Sanskrit at Baroda (12 years);
(c) Political leadership in Bengal (5 years); and
(d) *Ashrama*-life at Pondicherry (40 years)

The present chapter is confined to the last phase only.

A Glimpse of the Pondicherry Phase

1.3.2 In 1914, Paul Richard, a French writer, came to Pondicherry with his wife Mira Richard, to collaborate with Aurobindo in the starting of the philosophical journal, the Arya (Review of the Great Synthesis). The aims of this journal were to give to the reader:

(i) A systematic study of the highest problems of existence;
(ii) The formation of a vast synthesis of knowledge, harmonizing the diverse religious traditions of humanity, occidental as well as oriental. Its method will be that of realism, at once rational and transcendental, a realism consisting of the unification of intellectual and scientific disciplines with those of intuitive experience.

1.3.3 But soon after the journal Arya was started, the First World War broke out and Richard and his wife returned to France. Aurobindo continued the journal, publishing therein the results of his meditations, thoughts and experiences. In the next six years he published many of his famous writings, including "Essays on the Gita." About his written works Aurobindo later said, "I have made no endeavor in writing, I have simply left the higher power to work."

1.3.4 In 1920, Mira Richard, returned from Europe to join Aurobindo in the spiritual work she had envisioned as needed by the world. Her role in the *Ashrama* gradually became crucial, because Aurobindo needed support to fulfill his global mission. With the help of Mira Richard (who became the Mother of the *Ashrama*), Aurobindo was able to give to the world the spiritual message representing the result of his *sadhana.* With the Mother in charge of the *Ashrama,* Aurobindo could devote all his time for preparing the physical earth plane for the new Supramental age, the Kingdom of Heaven on Earth. He wrote thousands of letters to his followers and also completed the epic "*Savitri*" (23, 806 lines of inspired poetry).

1.3.5 Following his retirement into a secluded portion of the Ashrama, Aurobindo faced accusations of escaping the harsh world of reality and suffering, and of retreating into a pleasant, painless, non-abrasive seclusion. Aurobindo clarified and pointed out that such accusations arose out of an "illusion" –

> "But what strange ideas again! – that I was born with a supramental temperament, and that I have known nothing of hard realities! Good God! My whole life has been a struggle with hard realities, from hardships, starvation in England and constant dangers and fierce difficulties continually cropping up here in Pondicherry, external and internal. My life has been a battle from its early years and is still a battle: the fact that I wage it now from a room upstairs and by spiritual means as well as others that are external makes no difference in its character. But, of course, as we have not been shouting about these things, it is natural, I

suppose, for others to think that I am living in an august, glamorous lotus-eating dreamland where no hard facts of life or Nature present themselves. But what an illusion all the same!"[1]

1.3.6 In the world-wide message that Aurobindo sent on 15th August 1947, he spoke of his "dreams", which clearly showed how deeply devoted he always was to the ideals of "individual perfection, perfect society, human unity, and spiritual regeneration of the world."

"The first of these dreams was a revolutionary movement which would create a free and united India. India today is free, but she has not achieved unity..."

"Another dream was for the resurgence and liberation of the people of Asia and her return to her great role in the progress of civilization..."

"The third dream was a world-union forming the outer basis of a fairer, brighter and nobler life for all mankind...The momentum is there...A new spirit of oneness will take hold of the human race..."

"Another dream, the spiritual gift of India to the world has already begun...amid the disasters of the time more and more eyes are turning towards her with hope and there is even an increasing resort not only to her teachings, but to her psychic and spiritual practice..."

"The final dream was a step in evolution which would raise man to a higher and larger consciousness and begin the solution of the problems which have perplexed and vexed him since he first began to think and to dream of individual perfection and perfect society. This is still a personal hope and idea, an ideal which has begun to take hold both in India and in the West on forward-looking minds. The difficulties in the way are more formidable than in any other field of endeavor, but difficulties were made to be overcome."[2]

1.3.7 Aurobindo "withdrew from the physical body" on 5th December 1950. However, the Mother of the *Ashrama* continued implementing Aurobindo's ideas, two of which need special mention:

(i) Sri Aurobindo International University Center was started on 24th April 1951. It was later called 'Sri Aurobindo International Center of Education'.

(ii) Auroville, "the Cradle of a New World", was founded on 29th February 1968, a few miles from the *Ashrama* in Pondicherry. The idea is to demonstrate how a community might follow Aurobindo's ideals.

Formulation of Positive Philosophy

1.3.8 When Aurobindo was formulating "positive" philosophy, he noticed that Traditional *Vedantins* had not fully understood the Gita's teaching. We present below selected paragraphs from "Essays on the Gita" (in original form), that strengthened the practical Vedanta Movement.

Rejection of the *Jagat-Mithya* Doctrine

1.3.9 "The *Isha-Upanishad* tells us that *Brahman* is both the mobile and the immobile, is the One and the Many...It also insists like the Gita that man must know and must embrace both...But this greater knowledge and experience has still to get rid of a very real and pressing difficulty, a practical as well as a logical contradiction..."

"At first sight, the most persuasive conclusion would be that the mobility of the Spirit in Nature is an illusion...That is the familiar cutting of the knot of the riddle, *brahma satyam jagat-mithya...*"

"The Gita does not take refuge in this explanation...The Gita speaks of *Maya*, but only as a bewildering partial consciousness which loses hold of the complete reality, lives in the phenomenon of mobile Nature and has no sight of the Spirit of which she is the active Power, *me prakriti...*"

"When we transcend the Maya, the world does not disappear, it only changes its whole heart of meaning. In the spiritual vision we find not that all this does not really exist, but rather that all is, but with a sense quite other than its present mistaken significance: all is self and soul and nature of the Godhead, all is Vasudeva...The world for the Gita is real..."[3]

Positive versus Negative

1.3.10 "All existences are becomings of the Divine, *bhutani*; all subjective states and movements are his and their psychological becomings, *bhavah*...The Gita recognizes and stresses the distinction between Being and becoming, but does not turn it into an opposition...In the Transcendence, in the Absolute, if we are to follow the Gita, we must look, not for a supreme negation of all things, but for the positive key of their mystery, the reconciling secret of their existence."[4]

Escapism is Due to Incomplete Knowledge

1.3.11 "What then is the positive knowledge that will have to be admitted by the understanding, supported by the soul's faith and made real and living to the mind, heart, and life?"

"It is not by insisting on this or that side only of the truth that you can practice the yoga of the Gita..."

"If there were only the truth of an eternal impersonal self that neither acts nor creates, then the world and your soul would be illusions without any real basis. If you limit your faith and knowledge to this one lonely aspect, then renunciation of life and action would be your only resource..."

"But God in the world and you in the world are realities; the world and you are true and actual powers and manifestations of the Supreme. Therefore accept life and action and do not reject them..."[5]

***Lokasamgraha* Verses of the Gita (Chapter 3)**

1.3.12 "There are few more important passages in the Gita than the seven striking couplets, viz. *shlokas* 3.20 – 3.26..."

"*Janaka* and other great *karmayogins* of the mighty ancient *Yoga* attained to perfection, by equal and desire-less works done as a sacrifice, without the least egotistic aim or attachment:

Karmanaiva hi samsiddhim asthita janakadayah"

"So too and with the same desire-lessness, after liberation and perfection, works can and have to be continued by us in a large divine spirit, with the calm high nature of a spiritual royalty. Thou shouldst do works regarding also the holding together of the peoples;

Lokasamgraham evapi sampasyan kartum arhasi"

"Whatsoever the Best doeth, that the lower kind of man puts into practice; the standard he creates, the people follow. O Son of *Pritha,* I have no work that I need to do in all of the three worlds, I have nothing that I have not gained and have yet to gain, and I abide verily in the paths of action:

varta eva ca karmani eva

implying, I abide in it and do not leave it as the *samnyasin* thinks himself bound to abandon works. For if I did not abide sleeplessly in the paths of action, men follow in every way my path, these peoples would sink to destruction if I did not work and I would be the creator of confusion and slay these creatures.

"As those who know not, act with attachment to the action, he who knows should act without attachment, having for his motive to hold together the peoples. He should not create a division of their understanding in the ignorant who are attached to their works; he should set them to actions, doing them himself with knowledge and in Yoga."[6]

Karmayogins should be World-Workers

1.3.13 "The way of works is a far better release and a more perfect way and solution than the physical renunciation of life and works. A physical abstention is not entirely possible and is not in the measure of its possibility indispensable to the spirit's freedom, it is besides a dangerous example, for it exerts a misleading influence on ordinary men. The best, the greatest set the standard, which the rest of humanity strive to follow.

"Then, since action is the nature of the embodied spirit, since works are the will of the eternal Worker, the great spirits, the master-minds should set this example. World – workers should they be, doing all works of the world without reservation-God-workers, free, glad and desire-less, liberated souls and natures."[7]

***Karma-samnyasa* Ruled Out**

1.3.14 The *Avatara's* explicit message is:

> "I am the eternal Worker within you and I ask of you works. I demand of you not a passive consent to a mechanical movement of Nature from which in your self you are wholly separated, indifferent and aloof, but action complete and divine, done as the willing and understanding instrument of the Divine, done for God in you and others and for the good of the world. This action I propose to you, first no doubt as a means of perfection in the supreme spiritual Nature, but as a part too of that perfection. Action can and should be continued even after perfection and freedom are won. I ask of you the action of the *Jivanmukta.* Social responsibilities always remain."[8]

1.3.15 Summary of Aurobindo's contribution to Practical Vedanta

(a) He rejected the *jagat-mithya* doctrine of Shankaracharya
(b) He rejected the *karma-samnyasa* message of Shankaracharya
(c) His "Auroville" project contributed to the process of making Vedanta practical
(d) His book "Essays on the Gita" was a very valuable addition to Gita-literature

Endnotes

[1] Joan Price, *An Introduction to Sri Aurobindo's Philosophy*. Pondicherry, Second edition, 1982, pp. 18-9

[2] Karan Singh, *Prophet of Indian Nationalism*. George Allen and Unwin, London, 1963, pp. 155-6

[3] Sri Aurobindo, *Essays on the Gita*, Sri Aurobindo Ashram, Pondicherry, Ninth impression, 1989, pp. 425 - 6

[4] *Ibid*, p. 335

[5] *Ibid*, pp. 557 - 8

[6] *Ibid*, pp. 127 - 8

[7] *Ibid*, pp. 568 - 9

[8] *Ibid*, p. 566

CHAPTER 1.4

Tagore's Mission to make Vedanta Universal

1.4.1 Biographers of Rabindranath Tagore usually begin with his famous grandfather, Dwarkanath, who was called a "Prince" when he visited England. Side by side with his substantial business activities, he supported the social reformer, Ram Mohun Roy.

1.4.2 Tagore's father, Debendranath, was called "Maharshi", in recognition of his spiritual achievements. Vivekanada had called on him, seeking advice (before he met his Master, Ramakrishna Paramhans).

1.4.3 Rabindranath's brothers (who were themselves writers/artists) spotted in the young boy a keen interest in verse-writing, and they encouraged him to start writing when he was quite young. Thompson is awe-struck by the exceptional artistic talent of all the members of Tagore's family:

> "Music and drama were tne air he breathed. He has told us of the way his eldest brother entranced the household with the poetical opulence of his 'Dream-Journey', and of the way his fourth brother improvised melody after melody. The women were hardly less gifted, and were certainly not less eager."[1]

1.4.4 In his "Reminiscences", Rabindranath has left some desultory notes on his first appearances in print. These occurred before he was fifteen. Thompson explains how his brother promoted his literary activity:

"His brother Jyotirindra launched many projects, among them a line of patriotic (i.e. Bengali-owned and run) steamers, and a monthly, the "Bharati". The latter enterprise had the boy-poet as one of the crew, and for long enough it was his medium of expression, so much so that his first fifteen years of literary activity might be called the Bharati period."[2]

1.4.5 Thompson notes that Rabindranath was only sixteen when his talent as a writer of prose came to light:

"His 'Letters of a Visitor to Europe' are fresh and free from pose. His prose-writing skill was displayed in these letters. Then there was a famous assault on Michael Dutt's 'Meghnadbadh'. It is vigorous and acute. Rabindranath has always been the most independent critic of literature in Bengal, and one of the very few whose opinions have reason behind them."[3]

1.4.6 Further diversification in his literary career took place with the publication of a novel "*Karuna*", and a blank verse tragedy "*Rudrachandra*". This "gloomy" period reached its climax in his lyrical drama "*Bhagna-Hridaya*", about which Rabindranath wrote in his "Reminiscences":

"When I began to write 'Bhagna-Hridaya'. I was eighteen. Curiously, everyone around me seemed to be eighteen likewise; and we all flitted about in the same baseless, substance-less world of imagination, where even the most intense joys and sorrows seemed like the joys and sorrows of dreamland. This period of my life was one of utter disorderliness."[4]

1.4.7 Luckily, the "disorderly" years were followed by a period of intellectual ferment and literary experiment. Thompson saw clear signs of Rabindranath's transition:

"A break in his mood was provided by two musical comedies: '*Balmiki Pratibha*' and '*Kal Mrigaya*'. To the musical comedies he gave a rapture, which he tells us

> has never gone to the making of any other work of his. When '*Balmiki Pratibha*' was written, his house was a fountain of song."[5]

1.4.8 The age of thirty marks Rabindranath's entry into "worldly life". His father suggested that he should go to *Shelidah* and manage the family estates. At first, he was a little afraid, but at last he consented.

1.4.9 Rabindranath spent about ten years as "Manager". Two aspects of this phase are brought out in "*Chhinnapatra*". The first was: his desire to do something to help the poor villagers. In his own words:

> "My work as Zamindar took me on long distances from one village to another. In this way, I saw all aspects of village life. Slowly but surely, I began to understand the sorrow and the poverty of the villagers, and I grew restless to do something about it."[6]

The second aspect was: non-cooperation from the villagers themselves. Again, in his own words:

> "I had built a road from our estate office up to Kushtia. I told the villagers who lived close to the road. ' The upkeep of this road is your responsibility.' They replied, 'Must we look after the road so that gentle folk from Kushtia can come and go with ease?' I was deeply disappointed."[7]

1.4.10 In the early years of the twentieth century, Rabindranath became associated with anti-partition movement. He traced it to a divisive decision taken by the British:

> "The moment Lord Curzon's order was issued that Bengal would be divided, there arose from east to west one single cry that all Bengalis are one. When the pain of division became intolerable, we thought we would find redress if we made an appeal to the king. We did not know then that there were other ways, too, open to us."[8]

"Stirred by these developments, he plunged into the *Swadeshi* Movement, and contributed several patriotic songs to it. He even took part in street processions. But he was shocked when the movement degenerated and broke into violence."[9]

1.4.11 Although his "worldly activities" ran into difficulties, his literary activities moved up to great heights. The year 1901 saw the revival of the monthly "*Bangadarshan*", under the editorship of Rabindranath. His novel "Gora", which appeared a few years later, was acclaimed as 'the greatest novel in Bengali'. In 1908, a collected edition of his prose moved towards completion. He wrote a series of symbolic dramas. His religious poetry, expressing *Vedantic* ideas into melodious Bengali, rose to great heights. The original Bengali version of *Gitanjali* appeared in 1909.

1.4.12 As soon as the English version of *Gitanjali* came out, his fame spread over America and Europe. In 1913, he was crowned before the whole world with the Nobel prize for literature.

1.4.13 *Gitanjali* gave the message of peace and freedom:[10]

> "Where the mind is without fear and the head is held high;
> Where knowledge is free;
> Where the world has not been broken up into fragments by narrow domestic walls;
> Where the mind is led forward by thee into ever-widening thought and action;
> Into that heaven of freedom, my father, let my country awake."

1.4.14 Although Europe read *Gitanjali*, it headed towards World War I. Rabindranath was surprised to discover that some powerful sections in Europe were even suspicious of his message of peace, because he spoke out against militant nationalism.

1.4.15 At this point, we take a look into Rabindranath's great contribution in the field of education. In 1901, he founded the *Shantiniketan*, beginning with five students only. The initial period was difficult, as he wrote to C.F. Andrews, a great admirer of Tagore:

> "I sold all my books, my copyrights, everything I had, in order to carry on with the school. I can not really tell you what a struggle it was, and what difficulties I had to go through. At first, the object in view was purely patriotic, but later on it grew more spiritual... Because the growth of the school was the growth of my life and not that of a mere carrying out of my doctrines, its ideals changed with its maturity like a ripening fruit that not only grows in its bulk and deepens in its color, but undergoes change in the very quality of its inner pulp."[11]

1.4.16 With the War of 1914-18 in the West and the political conflicts in India, Rabindranath was in no doubt about the need for global cooperation. On 22 December 1918, he called a special meeting of students, teachers and well-wishers of the school at Shantiniketan, to explain his ideas about creating an institution for East-West fellowship and the study of cultures. The name *Vishva-Bharati* dates from that time and also its motto '*yatra vishvam, bhavati ekanidam*', taken from the *Vedas*, meaning, "where the world meets in one nest". During 1920-21, he went to Europe and America to raise funds and to enlist support for the institution. With Professor Sylvain Levi of Sorbonne University accepting his invitation to come as a visiting professor, the institution got off to a brilliant start.

1.4.17 In 1923, the Lecture Association of Peking invited him to China. Rabindranath gave lectures in the cities of Shanghai and Peking as well as in five of the country's twenty-four provincial capitals. From China, he went to Japan. The first international student at *Shantiniketan* had earlier come from Japan – a student of Sanskrit, named Hori San.

1.4.18 On his return from China and Japan, Rabindranath stayed home barely two months before he was travelling again.

This time he went to South America. The most memorable part of this trip was his visit to Argentina, where he was received by the famous writer and activist, Victoria Ocampo. This is what she wrote about this event:

"In September 1924, it was announced that Tagore would pass through Buenos Aires on his way to Peru. This was great news for those of us who knew his poems, in English, French, and Spanish. So we anxiously awaited his arrival, which for us would be the great event of the year."[12]

1.4.19 During his visit to USA, Rabindranath gave his message through lectures. However, during his visit to Ceylon, students of *Vishva-Bharati* staged his dramas. He also visited Persia and Iraq.

1.4.20 In the course of "The Nobel Prize Acceptance Speech", Rabindranath told the distinguished gathering of scholars from all over the world:

> "I want to assure you that the prize, which you have awarded to me, was not wasted upon myself. I have used this money for establishing and maintaining the university, which I have started. I invite you to come and join hands with us and not to leave this institution merely to us. Let your students and learned men come to us, and help us make this university a common institution for the East and the West. May we all together make it a true representative of the undivided Humanity of the world."[13]

1.4.21 We mentioned earlier that Japanese scholars joined hands with Rabindranath in developing *Shantiniketan*. But the situation changed in the thirties. The Japanese military machine invaded China, and even Japanese scholars supported this. In 1938, Rabindranath appealed to his friend, Yone Noguchi, to reconsider the matter calmly:

> Please take the risk and speak against Japan's aggression, as you have done against Italy's aggression. Please view this conflict as a temporary digression from the long-term trend. Let us hope, the Japanese and

Chinese people will soon join hands together, in wiping off memories of a bitter past. True Asian Humanity will be reborn. Poets will raise their song and will be unashamed to declare, fearlessly, their faith in a human destiny which cannot admit of a scientific mass production of fratricide."[14]

Spreading *Vedantic* Messages All Over the World

1.4.22 Tagore's "*Gitanjali*", after the award of Nobel Prize, helped spread *Vedantic* messages all over the World. The message of one-ness of all beings was beautifully conveyed through hymn no. 63:

"When one knows Thee,
Then alien there is none,
Then no door is shut.
Oh, grant me my prayer
That I may never lose
The bliss of the touch of the one
In the play of the many."

Through hymn no. 10, he tried to awaken sympathy towards the poorest members of the society:

"Pride can never approach
to where Thou keepest company
with the companion-less
among the poorest, the lowliest, and the lost."

1.4.23 "Tagore's deepest regret, when he approached the date of his death in 1941," writes Uma Das Gupta, "was that his work of village reconstruction could not remove social injustice. He put his absolute faith in Gandhi's leadership to help the destitute millions."[15]

1.4.24 Summary of Tagore's Contribution to Practical Vedanta

(a) During the first forty years of the 20th century, he was a major contributor to the cause of world peace (i.e. to Practical Vedanta)

(b) His Nobel-Prize winning book "*Gitanjali*", was a valuable addition to the world's *Vedantic* literature

(c) He established *Shantiniketan* and *Vishva Bharati* University to continue doing the work that he had started.

(d) He tried his best to help the poor.

Endnotes

[1] Edward John Thompson, *Rabindranath Tagore: His Life and Work.* Oxford University Press, 1921, pp. 7-8
[2] *Ibid.*, pp. 9-10
[3] *Ibid.*, p. 12
[4] *Ibid.*, p.13
[5] *Ibid.*, p.14
[6] Uma Das Gupta (ed.), *Rabindranath Tagore: My Life in My Words,* Penguin Books, 2010, p. 99
[7] *Ibid.*, p.109
[8] *Ibid.*, p.13
[9] *Ibid.*, p. 148
[10] Rabindranath Tagore, *Gitanjali.* KBS/Visva – Bharati. Eighth reprint, 2005, p.35
[11] Uma Das Gupta (ed.), *Rabindranath Tagore, op. cit.*, pp. 137-8
[12] *Ibid.*, p.227
[13] Rabindranath Tagore, *Gitanjali, op.cit.*, pp. 295-340
[14] Uma Das Gupta (ed.), *Rabindranath Tagore, op.cit.*, pp. 295-8
[15] *Ibid*

CHAPTER 1.5

Gandhi's Multi-Dimensional Contributions

1.5.1 Mohandas Karamchand Gandhi (or Gandhi for short) was born on 2nd October 1869. His schooling till High School was mainly in Rajkot. Two plays – the Filial Love of *Shravana*, and The Devotion to Truth of Harish Chandra – which Gandhi witnessed during his boyhood left an indelible impression in his mind. The reason why he called his autobiography as "The Story of my Experiments with Truth" can be traced back to the ideal, which the legendary Harish Chandra upheld under all circumstances. As Gandhi himself says:

> "To follow truth and to go through all the ordeals Harish Chandra went through was the one ideal it inspired in me. I literally believed in the story of Harish Chandra. The thought of it all often made me weep. My common sense tells me today that Harish Chandra could not have been an historical character. Still both Harish Chandra and *Shravana* are living realities for me, and I am sure I should be moved as before, if I were to read these plays again today."[1]

1.5.2 Among other influences of a religious nature, which started in Gandhi's early life and which are highlighted by him in his autobiography, "tolerance for all branches of Hinduism and sister religions" is attributed to his father's close and friendly ties with Shiva worshippers as well as Jain monks. Sarma further says:

"Mohandas listened, in the presence of his father, to the reading of the Ramayana of *Tulsidas.* Naturally he was profoundly impressed and has come to regard *Tulsidas*'s book even today (1944) as the greatest book in all devotional literature. Also, at this time, a Gujarati stanza gripped his mind and heart, especially its concluding lines (which can be translated as):

But the truly noble know all men as one,
And return with gladness good for evil done.[2]

1.5.3 At the age of eighteen, Gandhi went to England to study law. Two things that he did there (in addition to his studies) are noteworthy:

(a) He became an active member of the Vegetarian Society
(b) He read Bhagavad-Gita, through the translation by Edwin Arnold, entitled "The Song Celestial"

1.5.4 Gandhi returned to India with a law degree in 1891. He tried to set up legal practice, but did not succeed. Consequently, he was in a state of profound depression, when a job offer came from Dada Abdulla and Co., a firm in Porbandar, which had business in South Africa. Gandhi gladly accepted this offer and sailed for South Africa in April 1893.

1.5.5 The twenty-one years (1893-1914) that Gandhi spent in South Africa are the most important from the viewpoint of the development of his personality. South Africans proudly say – He came here as a barrister, and we made him a Mahatma. For purposes of the present book, we will concentrate attention on how the *Ahimsa*-based technique of social action: viz., "*Satyagraha*" was "born" on 11th September 1906.

Birth of Satyagraha, and its First Successful Use

1.5.6 The Transvaal legislation making it obligatory for Indians to obtain a "certificate" by 31 July 1907, was called by the Indian community as "the Black Act", and they had decided not to submit to it and to suffer the consequences thereof, but not to resort to violence. In the beginning, this movement was described as "Passive Resistance". However, Gandhi saw that the English term "Passive Resistance" was misleading, because it did not correctly indicate the nature of the Indian movement. "Passive Resistance" was supposed to be the weapon of the weak, who would use methods of violence if and when they could use them. This term could not therefore be applied to the Indian Movement, which had denounced all violence in thought as well as deed, and which aimed at conquering untruth by truth, hatred by love, and violence by non-violence. Gandhi therefore offered a prize, through his journal 'Indian Opinion', for the person who would invent the most suitable Indian expression, in place of "Passive Resistance". Maganlal Gandhi suggested the word "*Sadagraha*", and Gandhi himself modified it to "*Satyagraha*".

1.5.7 With a view to obtaining the Indian population's compliance with the "Black Act", the Transvaal Government opened many offices for receiving applications and for issuing "certificates". However, volunteers of the Indian community dissuaded the would-be applicants by picketing, so much so that only 500 certificates could be issued, as against a target of 13,000. On the last day of registration, that is, 31st July 1907, a mass meeting of the Indian community was called at Pretoria, the capital of the Transvaal, The Government sent one of their officers to this meeting, to admonish the leaders not to break their heads against a stone wall. However, this type of warning only strengthened the resolve of the people who were determined not to be cowed down by threats, nor even by punishment.

1.5.8 Soon the Government sent a warning to Gandhi and to other leading members of the Indian community that they must either register themselves under the Act or leave the country or face arrest. Accordingly, Gandhi was arrested and sentenced to two months' imprisonment. This was his first experience of jail life. Within a week more than a hundred *Satyagrahi* prisoners joined Gandhi. With more and more Indians ready to go to jail, the Government offered a compromise, saying that if a majority of Indians register voluntarily, and not by compulsion, the Black Act would be repealed. The compromise was accepted by the leaders of the Indian community, and all the *Satyagrahi* prisoners were freed.

1.5.9 Gandhi faced opposition from some of the Indians, but he was able to remove such misunderstanding. The community as a whole again expressed full confidence in Gandhi's leadership. Now it was the turn of the Transvaal Government to repeal the Black Act, but General Smuts, the head of the Government, refused to honor the word that he had given at the time of the compromise. Gandhi, who had risked his life in making his countrymen register themselves voluntarily, was shocked, at this breach of faith. How could he face the Indian community after this, he asked himself. He addressed a letter to General Smuts, but got no reply. He then consulted the other leaders of the community and announced that, unless the Government acted by a specific date (16th August 1908) the certificates collected by the Indians voluntarily would be burnt, and "they would humbly and firmly take the consequences."

1.5.10 General Smuts called the message of the Indians an ultimatum sent to the Government by people who had no idea of its power. But the Indians too were determined to meet the challenge, as Sarma describes:

> "A public meeting was announced to be held two hours after the time limit, for the purpose of the ceremony of making a bonfire of the certificates. On the mosque ground of Johannesburg every inch of available place was filled by Indians of all classes. An iron cauldron of the largest size available in the market was brought and set up on a platform in the grounds for the burning of the certificates. As the meeting was about to commence, a volunteer who had been posted at the Telegraph Office arrived on a cycle with a telegram from the Government announcing their

inability to change their minds. The telegram was read to the audience, who received it with cheers, and who re-confirmed their determination to continue the *Satyagraha* struggle."[3]

South African "*Satyagraha*" Called a 'Model'

1.5.11 It took six more years of determined and difficult struggle, by the Indian community, under the leadership of Gandhi and his wife, to achieve success. In Spratt's opinion, the *Satyagraha* in South Africa could be called a 'model', not only because it was the first use of the new technique, but also because it stayed very close to the principles:

> "It was conducted against very heavy odds by poor and ignorant people – the majority indeed were illiterate – but there was hardly an instance of breach of the principles."[4]

1.5.12 Perhaps the greatest testimony of Gandhi's success as a *Satyagrahi* was the change of heart that was apparently brought about in the "so-called opponent", General Smutts. Verma quotes how Smutts became deeply conscious of the virtues of sincerety, unselfishness and humanism that he found in Gandhi. Smutts wrote:

> "However often we may differ from him, we are conscious all the time of his sincerity, his unselfishness, and above all, of his fundamental and universal humanity. He always acts as a great human, with deep sympathy for men of all classes and all races, and especially for the under-dog."[5]

Gandhi, the Mahatma's Unique Contribution in India

1.5.13 Gandhi returned to India in 1915, to join the freedom struggle, which was led by Tilak at that time. On the need for applying the Gita to win independence, Tilak and Gandhi were equally enthusiastic. However, Gandhi introduced *Ahimsa*, which made India's struggle unique.

The First Significant Step

1.5.14 The first significant step which Gandhi took in 1917 was the *Champaran Satyagraha.* About the importance of this campaign, Gandhi told Louis Fischer, about twenty-five years later:

> "That day in Champaran became a red-letter day in my life. This was my first act of civil disobedience against the British. It became the method by which India could be made free."[6]

Non-Violent Non-Cooperation Movement 1920

1.5.15 In September 1920, Gandhi moved the resolution on non-cooperation at the special session of the Indian National Congress. Lala Lajpat Rai, a close colleague of the late B.G.Tilak, presided over this session. After a long discussion among the delegates – numbering nearly three thousand – Gandhi won by a majority of two to one. By this resolution, the Congress adopted the policy of progressive non-violent non-cooperation until the atrocities committed in the Punjab were acknowledged and corrective action taken to set them right and a policy of leading the country to *Swaraj* was announced.

1.5.16 Nehru believes that the full impact of the comprehensive scheme of withdrawal of cooperation went so deep as to shake up the very foundations of the British rule in India:

> "Realizing that the main props of British rule were fear, prestige, the cooperation, willing or unwilling, of the people, and certain classes whose vested interests were centered in British rule, Gandhi attacked these foundations. Titles were to be given up and though the title-holders responded to this only in small measure, the popular respect for these British-given titles disappeared and they became symbols of degradation. New standards and values were set up and the pomp and splendor of the vice-regal court

and the princes, which used to impress so much, suddenly appeared supremely ridiculous and vulgar and rather shameful, surrounded as they were by the poverty and misery of the people. Rich men were not so anxious to flaunt their riches; outwardly, at least many of them adopted simpler ways, and in their dress, became almost indistinguishable from humbler folk."[7]

Dandi-March and *Salt Satyagraha* 1930

1.5.17 In 1930, Gandhi picked up the issue of breaking the "Salt Tax Law" because this hurt the poorest of the Indians relatively more deeply. He envisaged a twenty-four day march from his *Ashrama* to the sea coast – known as the *Dandi March*– so that he could explain the idea personally to hundred of thousands of people and the message of civil disobedience could thus spread all over the country. Before starting the March, he addressed thousands of people who had gathered near Ahmedabad to receive his message. "Our case is strong, our means the purest and God is with us. There is no defeat for the Satyagrahis till they give up truth. I pray for the success of the battle which begins tomorrow."[8]

1.5.18 The twenty-four-day March by seventy-nine volunteers generated unprecedented enthusiasm and big support for the cause which Gandhi represented. The marchers reached Dandi on 5th April 1930, and next morning, Gandhi broke the salt law by picking up the salt from the sea-shore without paying tax, and added: "Now that the technical or ceremonial breach of the salt law has been committed, it is now open to everyone who would take the risk of the prosecution under the salt law to manufacture salt, wherever he wishes and whenever it is convenient."[9]

Sarma summarizes the events that followed: "This was the signal for huge demonstrations with tens of thousands of men and women in all the important towns of India. The whole country was ablaze with the fire of Civil Disobedience. The salt law was broken in many places. And there were pickets of foreign cloth shops and drinking booths by Satyagrahi women."[10]

1.5.19 The significance of *Dandi-March* was beautifully pointed out by Motilal Nehru:

> "Like the historic march of Ramachandra to Lanka, the march of Gandhi would be memorable, and the places he passes through would be sacred."[11]

Khadi (Hand-spun cloth)

1.5.20 *Khadi* – the hand-spun and hand-woven cloth – became a symbol of *Swadeshi*. Although there was initially some resistance from "modern" thinkers, poor villagers were happy to get some productive employment. Gandhi explained:

> "*Khadi* is a controversial subject. Many people think that in advancing *Khadi*, I am sailing against a head wind and am sure to sink the ship of *Swaraj* (self-rule), and that I am taking the country to the dark ages. But the proof of the pudding is in the eating. For me, nationwide spinning is a *yajna*. It is the symbol of unity of Indian humanity, of its economic freedom and equality, and, therefore, ultimately, in the poetic expression of Jawaharlal Nehru, "the livery of India's freedom."[12]

Abolition of Untouchability

1.5.21 The 1930's and the 1940's saw increasing attention paid by Gandhi as well as the Congress to tackle the problem of untouchability. Betai explains how Gandhi tried to meet the challenge posed by orthodox priests:

> "The Gita told him that all men and women are equal. Therefore he pleaded again and again that untouchability is a blot on Hindu society and religion. Vinoba Bhave faced *lathi-blows*, and Gandhi himself had to go on fast."[13]

Inter-Communal Harmony

1.5.22 The "divide-and-rule" policy of the British administration encouraged Muslims not to integrate themselves with the other communities. Louis Fisher explains how Gandhi tried his best to bring about peace:

> "The fact that Gandhi's fast restored Calcutta to its senses, the fact that his presence reduced the mass killing in Delhi to occasional outbursts, the fact that hardened bandits laid their arms at his feet – all this remains to inspire or haunt those whose actions suggest that they have forgotten the message of harmony. It is the seed of conscience and the source of hope."[14]

Constructive Program

1.5.23 Parallel to the 'agitation' element in the Satyagraha campaigns against the foreign rule, there was the 'internal growth' element to which Gandhi gave the meaningful name, "Constructive Program". Gandhi attached the greatest importance to the various activities which were included in the constructive program. As of 1940, the importance of the following items was highlighted by Gandhi under this program:

(i) Hindu-Muslim or communal unity
(ii) Removal of untouchability
(iii) Prohibition
(iv) Khadi
(v) Other village industries
(vi) Village sanitation
(vii) New or basic education
(viii) Adult education
(ix) Uplift of women
(x) Education in hygiene and health (including vegetarianism)
(xi) Propagation of *rashtrabhasha* i.e. national language
(xii) Cultivating love of one's own language
(xiii) Working for economic equality

1.5.24 Summary of Gandhi's contribution to Practical Vedanta:

(a) He moulded Gita's use for the freedom struggle, into a *Vedantic* act, by introducing *Ahimsa*.

(b) He supported demands for human rights, provided they are non-violent.

(c) He set an example for the whole world, how the military might of an Empire can be successfully challenged by non-violence. United Nations declared 2nd October as International Day of Non-Violence.

(d) He gave the *Vedantic* message that world peace cannot be established through wars.

(e) He demonstrated that the struggle against discrimination can be successfully conducted by non-violent means, in all countries. Leaders like Martin Luther King were inspired by him.

(f) He declared that untouchability is inconsistent with Vedanta. He risked his life for this cause, facing stiff resistance from orthodox people

(g) He demonstrated that women can play an important role in non-violent struggles for just causes.

(h) He helped in advocating and convincing people that anti-poverty programs deserve whole-hearted support.

(j) He helped in securing for India, a respectful view from world leaders.

(k) He helped in securing for Hinduism, a respectful view from other religious leaders.

(m) He sacrificed his life for promoting inter-religious harmony

(n) He supported vegetarianism, not only on health grounds, but also as a spiritual practice.

(p) His Gita-commentary was a very valuable addition to Gita-literature.

Endnotes

1 M.K. Gandhi, *The Story of My Experiments with Truth,* Beacon Press, Boston, p.7

2 D.S. Sarma, *The Renaissance of Hinduism, op.cit.* p.408

3 *Ibid.,* p 449

4 Raghavan Iyer, *The Moral and Political Thought of Mahatma Gandhi.* Oxford University Press, New York, 1978, p.326

5 V.P. Verma, *The Political Philosophy of Mahatma Gandhi and Sarvodaya.* Laxmi Narayan, Agra, 1959, p.59

6 D.S. Sarma, *The Renaissance of Hinduism, op.cit.,* p. 480

7 Jawaharlal Nehru, *The Discovery of India.* Oxford university Press, New Delhi, 1983 (third impression), p. 361

8 D.S. Sarma, *The Renaissance of Hinduism, op.cit.,* p. 532

9 *Ibid.,* p.533

10 *Ibid.,* p. 533

11 Raghavan Iyer, *The Moral and Political Thought of Mahatma Gandhi, op.cit.,* p.275

12 Shriman Narayan (ed.), *The Selected Works of Mahatma Gandhi* (Six Volumes). Navajivan, Ahmedabad, 1970

13 R.S. Betai, *Gita and Gandhiji.* Gujarat Vidyapith, Ahmedabad, 1970

14 M.M Verma, *Gandhi's Technique of Mass Mobilization.* R.K. Gupta, New delhi, 1990, p.207

CHAPTER 1.6

Meeting the Challenges of the 21st Century[1]

—Will Tuttle

1.6.1 Social injustice, war, hunger, environmental degradation, and the other problems we're facing are the direct result of the cultural attitudes and practices. Is there an idea that could transform the roots of our culture and create a solid foundation for peace, abundance, and sustainability? I believe there is, and that it has to do with questioning the pervasive influence of animal agriculture. Our culturally mandated daily food choices drive an industrialized killing machine of epic proportions that reaches its damaging tentacles into every cranny, not just of our Earth, but of our culture, our bodies, and the inner landscape of our attitudes, beliefs, assumptions, thoughts, and feelings. Both our outer world and our inner mentality reflect the food choices that are instilled in us from infancy.

1.6.2 Our most immediate and socially significant connection with the larger order is through eating food. Our food choices are a surprising and overlooked key to understanding our culture and ourselves, and to transforming our world toward harmony and freedom. The ripples of our mistreatment of animals for food are vast. The essential dot-connecting we are called to make today is between our routine abuse of animals and virtually all of the crises we face, both collectively and individually. In many ways, this is our basic intelligence test and, though it is obvious we've been flunking it for quite a while, it appears that the tide may be turning. We may be emerging from the culturally inflicted trauma we've endured, and from the psychological numbing and trancelike consensus that keeps us oblivious to the programming that violates us from early childhood. This desensitization turns us into perpetrators, propelling us to indirectly (and often directly) attack non-human animals, the Earth, each other, and ourselves.

1.6.3 We are all born into a culture that forced us, virtually from birth, to eat the flesh and secretions of certain animals who are bred, confined, attacked, and killed for this purpose. Early on, we are injected with the habit of disconnecting the reality that is on our plate from the reality required to get it onto our plate. I believe that there is no greater taboo in this culture than honestly discussing this, and the pervasive negative ramifications of using animals for food and other products. The reason it is such a potent taboo is that, in our hearts, we yearn to live in a world of kindness and respect for all life, and we know better. We naturally feel a kinship with nonhuman animals, so we repeat to each other many hollow and inaccurate official stories to justify our relentless mistreatment of animals for food, such as the protein story, the calcium story, the taste story, the no-soul story, and the life-feeds-on-life story, but the main weapon in our ongoing oppression of animals is our learned disconnectedness: we simply turn away, focus elsewhere, and numb our feelings. All the primary institutions in our culture (religion, science, media, family, government, business, and education) cooperate to keep our catastrophic abuse of animals well hidden, ignored, trivialized, and accepted.

1.6.4 And catastrophic it is. Not just to the animals and ecosystems, but to us, as well. Wherever we turn, we see the chicken of our mistreatment of animals coming home to roost. First, let's look briefly at some aspects of the external devastation caused by eating animal-sourced foods.

External Consequences of Animal Agriculture

1.6.5 Predictably, the most forcibly ignored cause of climate destabilization is eating meat and dairy products. As several writers in this volume discuss, breeding millions of cows, sheep, pigs, and other animals for food is the greatest source of nitrous oxide and methane, which are many times more powerful than carbon dioxide as greenhouse gases. The science on this is unequivocal and, in fact, a study by the WorldWatch Institute concluded that livestock production is responsible for a shocking 51% of greenhouse gas emissions by all human activity, including energy production, transportation, and industry.[2]

1.6.6 Eating animals requires massive amounts of fossil fuel inputs, directly pumping carbon dioxide into the atmosphere. In the West, we transport over 70% of our corn, soybeans, alfalfa, oats, and other grains to animal confinement operations, pump water to irrigate these fields, manufacture millions of pounds of fossil fuel-based fertilizers and pesticides, and house and slaughter billions of animals yearly. The end result of all this is that while it takes only about 2 calories of fossil fuel to produce one calorie of protein from soybeans, and 3 calories for wheat and corn, it takes roughly 54 calories of fossil fuel to produce one calorie of protein from beef. We waste huge amounts of petroleum for our meat and cheese, destabilize and overthrow foreign governments, and send our children to war to ensure supply.

1.6.7 On top of this, the primary driving force behind deforestation is cattle grazing and clearing land to grow soybeans and cereal grains to feed farmed cows, chickens, pigs and fish. This is a further major contributor not just to world hunger, global warming and climate destabilization, but also to the destruction of genetic diversity. By conservative estimate, we are destroying roughly an acre per second of Amazonian rainforest for animal agriculture,[3] and this is not just cutting down trees but destroying complex ecosystems and habitat in the midst of the most devastating mass extinction of species in 65 million years. According to biologists, we are driving an average of between 50 and 300 species into extinction every day,[4] and the driving force behind this is our collective action of taking out our wallets and paying for millions of pounds of meat, fish, dairy products, and eggs daily.

1.6.8 Two thirds of our fish are now factory-farmed, causing severe water pollution and decimating wild fish populations. Our seemingly limitless appetite for fish for feeding not just ourselves but farmed fish, birds, and mammals as well has brought our oceans to the brink of collapse. Dairy cows, for example, consume enormous quantities of fish, added as fishmeal to "enrich" their feed in order to increase milk and fat output. And it takes 3 to 5 pounds of caught fish to make one pound of farmed salmon. We have exterminated fishes, turtles and marine mammals and birds so completely that jellyfish are now taking over large areas of the oceans, and fishing vessels have to go so far out that they use unsustainable amounts of diesel fuel.[5] A study published in the prestigious *Lancet* medical journal concluded that the only effective way to reduce greenhouse gasses is to reduce human consumption of animal foods[6].

1.6.9 This is just the tip of the iceberg. Converting precious land, water, petroleum, and grains to animal fat, protein, and sewage is extravagantly wasteful, and is also the main driving force behind water pollution, topsoil loss, and habitat destruction. Eating animal-sourced foods is also inherently elitist. With our higher incomes, we buy grain and feed it to animals whose flesh and secretions we eat, driving up the price of grain on world markets so that those less affluent and in less industrialized countries suffer malnutrition and starvation. Thich Nhat Hanh has summed it well: "Everyday, forty thousand children die in the world for lack of food. We who overeat in the West, who are feeding grains to animals to make meat, are eating the flesh of these children."[7]

1.6.10 The information is available, and if we're interested, we can do the research and discover that a diet based on animal foods is responsible for the most serious environmental problems we face, and that it also devastates our personal environment as well as our social environment. The largest human nutrition study to date, the Cornell-Oxford study, concluded, "Our study suggests that the closer one approaches a total plant-based diet, the greater the health benefit."[8] Animal fat, animal protein, and cholesterol are directly implicated in the diseases that are epidemic in Western cultures such as heart disease, diabetes, obesity, strokes, kidney, liver, and gall bladder disease, breast, prostate, and colon cancer, arthritis, diverticulitis, autoimmune diseases, dementia, and so forth.

Internal and Historical Consequences of Animal Agriculture

1.6.11 Eating animal foods also devastates our social, psychological, and spiritual environment, because it fosters an attitude of reductionism, domination, disconnectedness, and exclusiveness. It is forced on us from infancy and is based, at its living core, on viciously dominating the reproductive cycles of female mammals, birds, and fishes. It requires a merciless exploitation of what we know in our bones is the most sacred dimension of life: mothers giving birth, nurturing, and protecting their offspring. Female animals are virtually always impregnated with sperm guns and restraining devices, their babies stolen from them and killed, and the mothers (mere "breeders") are also killed for their flesh after a few years of cruel exploitation. We drug them, we rape them, we terrorize them, we sicken them, we oppress them, we imprison them, we torture them, we break their families, and we wonder why we find pandemics of drugs, rape, terror, disease, oppression, incarceration, torture, and family breakdowns in our human world. As we sow, we reap. And we employ whole armies of our brothers and sisters to do the horrific work of confining, mutilating, and killing billions of hapless animals, work that brings out the worst in them. Slaughterhouse and animal farm workers have the highest rates of worker-related injuries, as well as suicide, drug addiction, alcoholism, spousal abuse, and violence. If we are ordering, buying, and eating these foods of death and despair, we are responsible. We forget what Martin Luther King, Jr., taught us – that injustice anywhere is a threat to justice everywhere. We are all connected.

1.6.12 From its beginnings about ten thousand years ago, animal agriculture has been a war against animals, nature, each other, and our basic wisdom and kindness. As free-living sheep, goats and later cows, pigs and other animals began to be enslaved and killed for food, other free-living animals began to be viewed as mere pests that potentially threatened the enslaved animals. Animal and nature were gradually reduced to commodities, and an insatiable demand for land, water, and food for the herds caused relentless and savage conflict among herders. A wealthy elite class emerged of the men who owned the most livestock, leading to the first full-scale wars, which were then, as they still are today, driven by the desire of the elites for more wealth and power. The first word for war that we know of, the ancient Sanskrit "*gavyaa*", means literally "the desire to own more cows".

1.6.13 The unfortunate losers of these first wars became the property of the victors, and so animal agriculture not only led to widespread warfare by herders against each other and against non-herders who were gardeners and gatherers. It also led to human slavery as well. Just as they impregnated female animals against their will to maximize their holdings and wealth, and castrated male animals to keep them docile, they learned to do the same to the human slaves they owned in order to maximize wealth and control.

1.6.14 The emergence of the practice of animal agriculture, which I refer to as the herding revolution in *The World Peace Diet,* is by far the most significant and devastating development in human history and pre-history, and yet it remains essentially invisible and unrecognized to this day. It occurred gradually over thousands of years, and it was a revolution of reductionism: reducing beings to the status of things. It required men whose innate sense of mercy and kindness was suppressed by routinely abusing nonhuman animals. Men are the natural role models for boys, traumatized by being forced to mutilate animals to become hard, tough men. Women were increasingly viewed as mere breeders to be impregnated and used by men, just like livestock, and the fascination among elites with bloodlines and the emergence of a rigidly hierarchical, patriarchal, and bellicose culture dominated by a few spread gradually throughout the Mediterranean, central Asia, Europe, and from there to the Americas, Africa, and virtually the entire planet today. It is the culture all of us are born into, and is at its core a herding culture. A competitive economic system based on ownership of capital (capital meaning "head" in ancient Latin, as in head of livestock), capitalism has encouraged the elite land-and livestock- owning class to control virtually every major institution in the warrior society that exits to this day, including government, media, religion, education, science, and business.

1.6.15 This system is a war against virtually all cultures, and all of us as individuals have been and continue to be traumatized by it. For example, as infants, we are forced not just to witness everyone around us eating the flesh of enslaved animals, but also to eat this ourselves and to betray our natural affection for animals. We are traumatized by the pervasive need to compete, and by being forced to witness violence in the media and often in our families, and to be routinely abused by the desensitized adults and by the culture into which we're born. Because we've been traumatized and thus numbed to violence, we willingly participate in systems of structural violence that inevitably traumatize nonhuman animals, ecosystems, and other people. This ongoing trauma leads to rampant social injustice and diminishes our natural capacity to create a world of equality, freedom, abundance, and sustainability.

Structural Violence, Institutionalized Injustice, and Attitudes of Domination

1.6.16 Structural violence leads to institutionalized injustice and internalized attitudes of domination. For example, the arising of the structural violence of animal agriculture led to the reduction of nonhuman animals to mere commodities to be owned, killed, and eaten, and fostered the justifying mentality of speciesism: that humans are inherently superior to animals.

1.6.17 Animal agriculture led directly to war, which led to the establishment of human slavery, as the victors, typically of a different ethnicity, tribe, and/or race than the vanquished, enslaved both the humans they defeated and their livestock. It is sobering to contemplate the basic truth that whatever we 've done to animals, we've also eventually done to each other. Thus, the structural violence of animal agriculture and war led to the structural violence of slavery, which led to the practice of domination and exploitation of people of other ethnicities and the justifying mentality of racism. Animal agriculture also directly led to the domination of the feminine as explained earlier, because female animals, particularly their reproductive organs and cycles, came under complete domination by male pastoralists, leading to the devaluation and exploitation of women who also eventually were seen as mere breeders to be used sexually and a property. The justifying mentality of sexism is the ongoing result of this institutionalized repression of females and the feminine, as required by animal agriculture. Similarly, animal agriculture requires boys to emulate the role model of the tough, hard, emotionally disconnected man, and the structural violence of socializing boys to be competitive and cruel towards other boys and animals and to use girls for sexual pleasure creates rigidity, harshness, and also mistrust and persecution of gay people and those who are "different" or less able to compete, and the resultant justifying mentalities of heterosexism and ableism.

1.6.18 Additionally, animal agriculture has always engendered an elite class of land and capital owners, and this structural violence leads to gross inequity in wealth and power, with the corresponding mentalities of classism, elitism, privilege, and entitlement. People who have less wealth and power suffer disproportionally from environmental degradation such as polluted and scarce water, air pollution, climate destabilization, and soil erosion, as well as from hunger, war, trafficking, and disease. Even more exploited are the free-living animals who are hunted, trapped, trafficked, and forced into starvation and extinction.

1.6.19 Animal agriculture is the unrecognized spinning fury at the core of both the outer and inner domains of exploitation, traumatizing the Earth, other species, our culture, and the inner landscape of our emotions and attitudes. It reaches also into plant agriculture as well. Because animal agriculture has completely insinuated its norms into our lives, we engage in plant agriculture – which is essentially harmonious and working with the bounty of seeds, gardens, and life-affirming abundance—the way we engage in animal agriculture, which is essentially about enslaving, killing, and dominating by force. So we see the perverse deployment of GMO crops, toxic pesticides and chemical fertilizers, monocropping, and other practices that turn plant agriculture into a war against nature and an effort to dominate the Earth and the feminine, conducted in the same way we engage in animal agriculture. In every other arena, the same mentality is applied. Another obvious example is health care, which in the dominant medical paradigm is seen as a war against nature, bacteria, and viruses using weapons and technologies of violence, rather than seeing our health as a reflection of our feelings, attitudes, and relationships with nature and each other.

1.6.20 Over the past 20 years or so, it has become clear that children who are traumatized, and who cruelly practice torturing and killing animals, are likely to become dangerous to other people as they get older. It's now well understood that serial killers practice first on animals. As we work to heal the many social justice issues we face, it is incumbent upon us to look deeply into the roots of our violence toward each other, and to question both the practice and the mentality required by animal agriculture. It's well understood now that one of the worst things we can do to a child is to let him or her get away with cruelty towards animals. The same is true of ourselves. Working for peace, justice, sustainability, and equality without questioning animal agriculture is addressing symptoms while ignoring the underlying cause.

The Cultural Transformation is at Hand

1.6.21 Veganism – striving to minimize our violence and injustice toward others – is indeed an idea whose time has come. The beauty of veganism is that it reflects our true nature, and it is not just a philosophy, but also requires a basic transformation in our way of living. Veganism is nothing to be proud of. It is simply our true human eyes looking out and seeing beings to be respected rather than commodities to be manipulated and used for selfish purposes. The motivation underlying veganism is compassion and justice for all, and as each of us awakens to the power of this idea and begins to live it, we directly reduce animal cruelty and suffering. We bless the world by dramatically reducing our abuse of the Earth, other humans, other species, our loved ones, and ourselves. Our physical, psychological, social, and spiritual health are all connected, and they can flourish when we understand and live this understanding.

1.6.22 Strong diseases demand strong medicine. Veganism, properly understood, is that medicine, and it can be practiced by any one of us, starting right this minute. Authentic vegan living fundamentally questions and rejects the deep-seated, culturally-mandated attitudes of exclusivism, reductionism, and disconnectedness that generate our unyielding dilemmas. It replaces them with inclusion, compassion, respect, and awareness. Our culture will go vegan, transform, and flourish, or it will continue brutalizing animals, humans, and the Earth to its self-destruction. We are not the only species on this planet, and we cannot continue to usurp the wisdom of the web of life here.

1.6.23 I have sketched just the briefest of outlines in this short piece. Today, perhaps more than ever before, we are in the position to recognize, understand, and discuss at a global level the devastating role animal agriculture plays in our lives, and to transform both our individual and collective lives with this understanding and discussion. Imagining a vegan world is imagining a completely different reality, immeasurably more sane, just, and in harmony with our true nature.

1.6.24 To understand the deep structure of our culture and the big picture in more detail, please read, explore, study, and ask questions. Each of us can change, and we are each called to be, as Gandhi said, the change we would like to see in the world. This is our vision and its message and power.

Endnotes

[1] This essay had earlier appeared in *"Circles of Compassion"* under the title "Unrecognized Roots of Injustice and the Vegan Transformation".

[2] Robert Goodland and Jeff Anhang, "Livestock and Climate Change," *World Watch* 22, no.6 (2009): 10-19, http://www. Worldwatch.org/files/pdf/Livestock%20and%20Climate%20Change.pdf.

[3] Editorial Board, "Losing Ground in the Amazon,"*The New York Times*, April 15, 2014, http:www.nytimes.com/2014/04/16/opinion/losing-ground-in-the-amazon.html?_r=1

[4] S.L. Pimm, G.J.Russell, J.L.Gittleman, and T.M.Brooks, "The Future of Biodiversity,"Science 269(1995):347-350.

[5] Elizabeth Kolbert, "Is there Any Hope for our Overfarmed Oceans?"*The New Yorker*, August 2, 2010.

[6] The Canadian Press, "Eat Less Meat, Reduce Global Heat, Says Study,"*CBCNews*, September 13, 2007, http://www.cbc.ca/news/technology/eat-less-meat-reduce-global-heat-says-study-1.644769.

[7] Thich Nhat Hanh, Creating True Peace (New York: Simon &Schuster, 2003), 77.

[8] Colin Campbell, interview 1994, cited in Andrea Wiebers and David Wiebers, Souls Like Ourselves (Rochester, MN: Sojourn Press, 200). 51

PART II

PRACTICAL VEDANTA

A Simplilfied Presentation

व्यावहारिक वेदान्त

सरल भाषा में

Part II

Practical Vedanta
A Simplified Presentation
(व्यावहारिक वेदान्त - सरल भाषा में)

Dedication (समर्पण)

Part II has twelve chapters. The first chapter summarizes how the Practical Vedanta Movement was started and how its scope was widened. The next eleven chapters (2nd through 12th) present 195 self-composed semi-poetic reflections. These are heart-felt expressions intended to promote the message of good-of-all, on various occasions during the last ten years. We are not poets, therefore we request readers to ignore grammatical shortcomings, and instead consider carefully, the usefulness and application of the message that we have tried to give.

To facilitate this, the Hindi version is accompanied with its meaning in simple English (not a translation).

We dedicate this humble offering, as advised by the Gita, to the Almighty.

पुस्तक के इस भाग में बारह अध्याय हैं। पहले अध्याय में व्यावहारिक वेदान्त के आरम्भ एवं विकास का संक्षिप्त विवरण है। दूसरे से बारहवें अध्याय तक (अर्थात् ग्यारह अध्यायों में) स्वरचित गद्य-काव्य की 195 रचनाएँ हैं। इन रचनाओं में पिछले दस वर्षों के विभिन्न अवसरों पर लिखी गई, सर्व-हित-भावना से प्रेरित, अन्तस्तल की पुकार है। तुलसीदास जी के शब्दों में -

"कवि न होउँ नहीं चतुर कहावउँ।"

इसलिए पाठकों से प्रार्थना है कि वे भाषा की त्रुटियों को न देखें, बल्कि भावों की उपयोगिता पर ध्यान केंद्रित करें।

पाठकों की सुविधा के लिए प्रत्येक रचना का सरल अंग्रेज़ी में (अनुवाद नहीं) भावार्थ लिखा है।

निष्काम - भाव से किए गए, इस प्रयास को हम प्रभु को समर्पित करते हैं। उनकी कृपा से ही पाठक व्यावहारिक वेदान्त में रुचि लेंगे।

CHAPTER 2.1

Practical Vedanta: Its Beginning and Steady Growth

(व्यावहारिक वेदान्त का आरम्भ एवं विकास)

2.1.1 व्यावहारिक वेदान्त का आरम्भ, स्वामी विवेकानन्द ने, 1896 में किया। कई वर्षों की पैदल यात्रा के फलस्वरूप उन्हें यह स्पष्ट हो गया कि वेदान्त के विद्वानों ने शूद्रों के कष्टों को दूर करने का कोई प्रभावशाली कार्यक्रम नहीं बनाया। यद्यपि वेदान्त दर्शन ने, सभी व्यक्तियों के प्रति समदृष्टि की शिक्षा दी थी, फिर भी उच्च वर्ण के लोगों का व्यवहार भेद-भाव-पूर्ण था, इसलिए ग़रीबों का शोषण हुआ। अर्थात् ज्ञान और व्यवहार में मेल नहीं था। इस चिन्तनीय स्थिति को ठीक करने के लिए स्वामी विवेकानन्द ने व्यावहारिक वेदान्त की स्थापना की।

2.1.2 स्वामी विवेकानन्द ने एक नया आर्षवाक्य लिखा -
"आत्मनो मोक्षार्थं जगद्-हिताय च"
अर्थात् व्यावहारिक वेदान्त जगद्-हित को प्राथमिकता देता है।

2.1.3 लगभग उसी समय लोकमान्य तिलक ने कहा कि जनता के कष्टों को दूर करने के लिए अंग्रेज़ी राज्य को हटाना आवश्यक है। श्री अरविंद ने स्वतन्त्रता-आन्दोलन में तिलक का साथ दिया। 1919 में जलियाँवाला हत्याकाण्ड के बाद महात्मा गांधी ने स्वतन्त्रता-आन्दोलन को अहिंसा-नीति के द्वारा नया रूप दिया। उन्होंने कहा कि वे भगवद्गीता के भक्त हैं और उनका सत्याग्रह व्यावहारिक वेदान्त का ही अंग है।

2.1.4 इस प्रकार व्यावहारिक वेदान्त के दो स्तम्भ हो गए
(1) जगद्-हित

(2) अहिंसा-योग से स्वतंत्रता-प्राप्ति

और देश की दो बड़ी समस्याओं को दूर करने पर ज़ोर दिया -

(1) छुआ-छूत

(2) ग़रीबी

2.1.5 धीरे-धीरे, व्यावहारिक वेदान्त ने अन्य विषयों को भी अपनाया -

(1) परस्पर-भाव, मेल-जोल

(2) महिलाओं की शिक्षा और उन्नति

(3) विश्वशान्ति

Practical Vedanta: Its Beginning and Steady Growth

2.1.1 Swami Vivekananda started the Practical Vedanta Movement in 1896. He walked on foot, for several years, all over India, which convinced him that Vedantic scholars did not pay enough attention to improve the miserable conditions of the poor. Although Vedantic philosophy had given the message of one-ness of all beings, it was not reflected in the day-to-day behavior of the scholars. Consequently, the upper castes exploited the lower castes, and even practiced untouchability. He knew that, to improve such a painful situation needed a long time effort. Swami Vivekananda started the process.

2.1.2 In 1897, Swami Vivekananda established Ramakrishna Mission, whose motto was *"atmano moksarthan jagad-hitaya ca"*, i.e. The monk's goal of life (which was moksha till then) will be "good of the world".

2.1.3 Ramakrishna Mission was a non-political organization. Lokmanya Tilak started the process of adding the political dimension to Practical Vedanta. He was supported by Sri Aurobindo, who also changed the 'negative philosophy' of Traditional Vedanta, into 'positive philosophy'. Nobel - Laureate Ravindranath Tagore spread the messages of Practical Vedanta all over the world, and also established Shanti-Niketan, his university of Creative Arts. Mahatma Gandhi introduced Ahimsa, or non-violence, and succeeded in achieving India's independence. He also succeeded in paving the way to abolish untouchability.

2.1.4 The multi-dimensional form of Practical Vedanta is presented in the next eleven chapters, in a simple style, presented in the form of poetic reflections.

CHAPTER 2.2

Seva - Yoga Based on Vedanta

(वेदान्त के माध्यम से सेवायोग का संदेश)

2.2.1 उन्नीसवीं शताब्दी के ऋषि

नमन करो स्वामी विवेकानन्द को। वेदान्त को व्यावहारिक रूप दिया
प्राथमिकता दी कर्मयोग को, देश-काल-पात्र का अर्थ सिखाया।
इतने गहरे विचारों को कितने सुन्दर ढंग से किया और कराया।।
कितना विवेक था, विवेकानन्द के कार्य और विचारों में।
आधुनिक समय में कितनी उपयोगी और हितकारी है उनकी शिक्षा।।
जगत्-हित का संदेश है उसमें, दरिद्र-सेवा है इसका लक्ष्य।
इन्हीं विचारों को लेकर इस पुस्तक का है जन्म हुआ।।

Nineteenth Century's Rishi
We bow to Swami Vivekananda —
He started the movement to make Vedanta practical
He emphasized Karma yoga
Presenting it as Sevayoga
His teachings are very useful in the present time
His aim was to enrich Vedanta with the message of good of all
Inspired by these ideas, we wrote our book on Practical Vedanta.

2.2.2 दरिद्र नारायण

देख दुखी की निर्धनता, विवेकानन्द का हृदय यूँ बोल उठा।
मन से करो इनकी सेवा, भर पेट इन्हें भोजन दो, सभी तरह से दो प्यार इन्हें।।
भक्ति, ज्ञान, ध्यान की शिक्षा सार्थक तभी जब मन में हो त्याग, प्रेम, निस्वार्थ कर्म भरा हुआ।

कोरा ज्ञान शुष्क है, जोड़ दो उसे प्यार, दया, और सरल भाव से।
ईश्वर रूप देख लो हर प्राणी में, सबसे प्रथम दरिद्र और अपाहिज में।।
वेदान्त के विचारों को बनाओ व्यावहारिक, सर्वहितकारी।

Seeing God in the Poor
Vivekananda appealed, help the poor with respect
Serve them with kindness, feed them well and love them whole-heartedly
Worship, meditation, knowledge, all are worthwhile only when your heart is full of sacrifice, love and selfless work
Fill your life with love, kindness and simplicity
See God, He is in everybody, and especially in the poor and disabled
Dharma of a practical Vedantin is Seva of daridra-narayana.

2.2.3 कर्म ही पूजा है

हर जीव में देखो ब्रह्म स्वरूप, वही है सच्चा नारायण रूप।
विवेकानन्द को दरिद्र में, दरिद्र नारायण दिए दिखाई।।
गाँधी ने सत्य अहिंसा में देखा सारा धर्म-कर्म।
तिलक ने लोकसंग्रह में पाया मानव-धर्म और सत्य विचार।।
टैगोर को प्रकृति में दिए खड़े भगवान् दिखाई।
नेहरू को देश-प्रेम ही लगा जीवन का परम-ध्येय।।
राधाकृष्णन ने सरस्वती माँ में पाया समस्त रहस्य जीवन का।
सबने की पूजा भिन्न तरह, इस तरह रहे कर्म-काण्ड से दूर सभी।।
जुटे रहे सब मानव-सेवा में, बनकर जीवनमुक्त इसी जीवन में।

Work is Worship
See divinity in everyone, see the reality called Brahman
Vivekananda saw divinity in the poorest beings
Gandhi realized religion and action in truth and non-violence
Tilak did his duty for the freedom of the country
Tagore found God in Nature
Nehru believed love towards the nation was his highest goal
Radhakrishnan saw reality in Saraswati, the goddess of learning
All these great people worshipped differently and kept themselves away from rituals

They all served humanity and became liberated in this very life.

2.2.4 कर्म बने पूजा मेरी

कर्म बने पूजा मेरी, 'सर्वहित' बने धर्म मेरा।
हर प्राणी में दीखे सूरत तेरी, दरिद्रों में हो ध्यान मेरा।।
सेवा प्रेरक जनक-पत्नी ने उच्च स्वर में कहा सुनो।
सेवा-संदेश अनुगीता में जो है पढ़ने योग्य सर्वैः।।

Work is Sewa
Anu - Gita's chapter seven gives a most inspiring message
Janak's wife's words are like Rishi's words
Let work be thy worship,
Let good-of-all be thy dharma
May we see God in every being
And particularly in the poor
Let sewa-yoga get the top priority

2.2.5 ऋषि अरविन्द

श्री अरविन्द ने शास्त्र रचा व्यावहारिक वेदान्त का।
स्वयं ने की गहरी साधना, जगत् को दिया ज्ञान पूर्ण योग का।।
ब्रह्म बसा है हर कण में, समस्त जगत् का है आधार।
मानव से करवाता सही काम, देता लोक-संग्रह का संदेश।।
निष्कपट, निःस्वार्थ रह कर, जीवन्मुक्त विचरते सबके बीच।
मानव, प्रेरणा उनसे पाकर, करता निःस्वार्थ जगत्हित के काम।।

Sri Aurobindo
Sri Aurobindo was a Rishi, he gave us the teaching of Purnayoga
He meditated deeply and gave new ideas to the world
The whole universe is Brahman-based and so is all activity in the world
The Almighty is active always (this is a departure from Shankaracharya's teaching)
Jivan-muktas have no enemy, and are busy doing good to all
Sri Aurobindo strengthened the Practical Vedanta Movement.

2.2.6 इच्छा

इच्छा है मन की मृग-तृष्णा, जितना पीछे भागे, उतनी ही आगे और बढ़ी।
रहस्य है इसमें भी एक बड़ा, छोड़ अपनी इच्छा, परहित की इच्छा पर जो दौड़ा।।
वह तो बस निःस्वार्थ हो कर्म में लगा रहा, निर्णय ईश्वर पर छोड़ा।
बड़े-बड़े महर्षि, साधु-सन्त हुए, समाज-सुधारक, नेता, ज्ञानी हुए।।
ईश्वर शक्ति उनमें अधिक है आई, सहर्ष आपत्ति झेली, कमज़ोरी कभी न आई।
वेदान्त को व्यावहारिक बनाया, देश, समाज को ऊँचा उठाया, स्वयं सभी का प्रेम है पाया।।

Desire

Desire is like a mirage, more you run after it, farther it is
But it can be made a virtue—leave your own selfish desire and have desire for the good of others
Such people are always busy in action and leave outcome to God
There have been great personalities, like social workers, leaders, scholars or saints
They receive divine support, they face difficulties gladly, and never show weakness
They are practical Vedantins—they try to uplift their country and society without any selfish motive
They get lot of love and appreciation and become role models

2.2.7 व्यवहारिक-ज्ञान और कर्म कुशलता

वेदान्त की मज़बूत नींव पड़ी, व्यवहार जगत् में बनी इमारत।
ज्ञान हुआ महा ग्रन्थों से, बाहरी जगत में हुआ प्रयोग।।
जिसको इन दोनों का अहसास हुआ, चेहरे पर चार चाँद लगे।
सफ़लता मिली हर क्षेत्र में उसको, देश-विदेश में सम्मान हुआ।।
कर्म-कुशलता वास्तविक योग है, 'गीता' ने सिखलाया है।

Practical Vedanta and Efficiency in Work

Vedanta is a strong foundation. Outer manifestation is like a beautiful building
Knowledge we have received from ancient scriptures; application is needed in the world around us

Those who have this understanding shine like many moons together
Such people receive success in everything they do, get respect everywhere
Gita declares again and again, it is the combination of both knowledge and application that is the essence of life

2.2.8 व्यावहारिक वेदान्त और आचरण

वेदान्त हमारी नैया है, हमको ज्ञान सिखाती, विश्वास जगाती।
नदियाँ पार तभी हैं होती, जब हाथ में पतवार हो कर्मठता की दृढ़ता की।।
जाप किये, लेकर रुद्राक्ष की माला, फूल चढ़ाए मन्दिर पर।
मन की माला कभी न फेरी, ना आए काम किसी के जीवन भर।।
अन्त में आया रोना, वेदान्त ने तो बहुत सिखाया था।
हमने उसका ना किया प्रयोग, ना ही समाज पर ध्यान जमाया था।।

Practical Vedanta and its Application

Vedanta is our canoe, which gives us knowledge and confidence
But we can only cross the river when we have oars of hard work and perseverance
Those who prepare garlands and count beads, take flowers to temples and holy places
But never care to turn the beads of their hearts, nor do they care to help others
They cry at the time of departure from earth, realizing that knowledge is wasted
Neither they make use of it in life, nor is it useful for society.

2.2.9 निडर कैसे बनें

आज संसार भयभीत हुआ है, अत्याचारों से, बम के गोले से, बच्चे बूढ़ों के एकाकीपन से।
भोले भाले, शाकाहारी पालतू जानवर डरे हुए हैं, सताए जा रहे हैं, खान-पान के ढंगों से।।
क्या समस्याएँ कभी सुलझी हैं, लड़ाई झगड़ा करके, बदला लेने से या बुरी तरह सताने से।

प्रेम, दया, भाईचारा जो है हर धर्म का मूल विचार, उसे अपनाओ और जीवन से लो जोड़।।
समस्त जीव और प्रकृति, हैं ईश्वर का उपहार जगत् को, निभाओ सब मिलकर इस धर्म को।
शांति स्थापित होगी, अच्छे संस्कार मिलेंगे, खुली हवा में निडर भाव से रहा करेंगे।।
यही है हमारा व्यावहारिक ज्ञान और सत्य-विचार।

How to Get Rid of Fear
At present, everybody is afraid of crimes, attacks and loneliness
Innocent, grass-eating animals are being harassed and killed due to bad habits of eating meat
Problems can never be solved by fights, revenge and harassment
Keep in mind love, kindness and brotherhood are the essence of all religions
With it we can establish peace, have a purposeful life, and can live fearlessly
This is our practical knowledge and healthy thinking.

2.2.10 धन और व्यवहार
धन और व्यवहार से जगत् के समस्त काम हैं होते।
धन सामान बटोरता, सैर कराता, सेवक घर में लाता है।।
व्यवहार आदर-भाव सिखाता और जोड़ता सबसे नाता है।
संसार वैर-भावना से भरा हुआ, लड़ाई-झगड़ों में है लगा हुआ।
दूर हुई है प्रेम भावना, त्याग नम्रता, स्वार्थ सिद्धि में है फँसा हुआ।
दोनों में जहाँ हुआ संतुलन, वहाँ सुख शांति का वास हुआ।।
व्यावहारिक वेदान्त की सीख यही, मिला जीवन में संदेश सही।

Behavior and Wealth
In this world, behavior and wealth are very important to solve today's problems
We buy every item with money, see places and keep helpers
Behavior unites us all and teaches us the right path of oneness
This world is full of enmity and fights, people do not care for other fellow's feelings

Selfish interests have become more important than love and kindness
We should always try to keep balance between the two
Practical Vedanta gives us the right message and takes us ahead in life.

2.2.11 दैवी शक्ति

हर प्राणी में है देवी-शक्ति, आत्मा सबमें विराज रही।
शक्तिहीन नहीं है कोई, अन्धकार से हैं घिरे हुए।।
इन्द्रियों पर जितना होता अधिकार हमारा, उतना ही दैवी रूप नज़र आता।
छोड़ आसक्ति, कमज़ोरी को, हिम्मत से कर सब काम।।
व्यावहारिक वेदान्त सिखाता, सर्वसुखी जीवन बनेगा, सफल होंगे सब काम।
ईश्वर सबके अन्दर है, रख पूर्ण विश्वास, भला सोच सदा सभी का।।

Divine strength
We all have Atman, which means everybody has divine strength
Nobody is weak, the problem is that we are living in darkness
There is more divinity in those, who have more control on their senses
We must leave attachment, weakness and move forward with courage and do our duties
Divinity will show more in life, we will be successful, this is what Practical Vedanta teaches
Always have confidence, think well of others, divinity is in everyone.

2.2.12 हृदय-मस्तिष्क का हुआ मिलन

मानव के हृदय-मस्तिष्क का हुआ गहन-मिलन,
व्यावहारिक वेदान्त का हुआ जन्म।
हाथों ने जैसी कला दिखाई, मुख से वैसे शब्द हैं निकले,
चेहरे पर शीतलता की लाली चमकी, आँखों में प्रेम की धारा टपकी।
मित्रों ने चारों ओर है घेरा डाला, सभी ने काम में हाथ बँटाया,
ना किसी की करी है निंदा, ना किसी का अनहित सोचा।
सभी मिले और एक बने, विचारों का आदान-प्रदान हुआ,
इसी को कहते मानवता, एक ने एक को मार्ग दिखाया।

हर कर्म का बीज हमारे अन्दर है, उसी से कर्म-वृक्ष पनपता है,
सावधानी का लिया सहारा, आगे आगे क़दम बढ़ाया।

Heart and Mind are United

As heart and mind become one, the beauty of action becomes visible
Hands do accordingly and we speak out the same way
We see peace on the face and eyes show love
Friends come and collectively help each other
We all love and nobody makes false criticism
We see oneness and exchange ideas
This is what we call Practical Vedanta
Everything comes from within, and it appears in the outer world
Always be careful and go forward.

2.2.13 व्यवहार का आधार

व्यवहार अन्तर जगत् से आता है, बाहरी रूप है परछाईं।
जैसी जिसकी रही भावना, वैसा ही रूप निखर कर आता है।।
वैसी ही वाणी होती, वैसा ही सौन्दर्य झलकता चेहरे पर।
नक़ल करने की वस्तु नहीं, निष्कपट, सरल-हृदय की सोच है यह।।
जिसका जितना अंकुश मन पर है, वैसा ही उसका व्यवहार हुआ।
व्यवहार उठाता ऊँचा है, व्यवहार हमारा गहना है, इसका रहे ध्यान सदा।।

Origin of Behavior

Behavior comes from inside ourselves; the outer manifestation is merely a shadow
Whatever you think inside, its expression appears and shows on your face
It is reflected in your words and in the way you conduct yourself
It cannot be copied; it is a reflection of your innocence, the feelings of your heart
Your behavior depicts your balance of mind
It brings you respect, uplifts and embellishes you.

2.2.14 हृदय-मस्तिष्क एक बराबर

तर्क - वितर्क मुझे न भाते, मैं भावों की रानी हूँ।
हृदय में जब भाव है उठता, सहारा मस्तिष्क का लेता है।।

मार्ग दिखाई देता है, क़दम आगे बढ़ जाते हैं।
कोरा मस्तिष्क लड़ाई - झगड़े लाता है, शुष्कता आ जाती है।।
दोनों में परस्पर मेल है होता, निर्णय सही हो जाता है।

Heart and Mind are Equal
I don't like dry arguments; I am the queen of sentiments
When you get thoughts in your heart, intellect strengthens them
We can clearly see our way and go forward intuitively
Dry logic brings unpleasant fights, and brings dryness in life
Right decisions come when the heart and the mind meet together.

2.2.15 दुःख की देन

दुःख को कभी न भूल सकूँगी, दुःख ने मुझको बहुत सिखाया।
सहन शक्ति दी है तूने, मान अपमान का भेद मिटाया।।
परिश्रम की क्षमता और बढ़ी, आपत्ति झेलने की सीख मिली।
कुन्ती ने भगवान् कृष्ण से कष्ट का वरदान था माँगा।।
जीवन भर कष्टों का किया सामना, गाँधी ने देश आज़ाद कराया।
दुःख ही हमको शिक्षा देता है, सच्ची सीख सिखाता है।।
इससे घबराना कैसा, यह तो सच्चा साथी है।

The Gift of Struggle and Suffering
Suffering is my teacher, taught me a lot, I can not forget it
Taught me tolerance, made me capable of facing insults and taunts
I worked harder and harder and learnt to face challenges more and more
Kunti asked Lord Krishna to bless her with gift of suffering
To make the country free, Gandhi suffered so much
Only struggle can teach us and take us to the right path
It is your greatest friend; never get frightened from it

2.2.16 गाँधी युग

बचपन जब याद है आता, 'गाँधी युग' की याद दिलाता है।
देश के बच्चे बच्चे का कैसे चरित्र उठाया था।।
सुबह उठो, निकलो ले स्वतन्त्रता का झंडा, करो गली गली की फेरी।
गर्दन तुम्हारी तनी रहे, निगाह झुकी रहे, चेहरा सदा शान्त रहे।

जो भी पथ में तुम्हें मिले सबको गले लगाते चलो।।
यह देश तुम्हारा अपना है, सभी तुम्हारे अपने हैं, किसी को दूसरा न कहो कभी।
रुको पथ में कभी नहीं, क़दम बढ़ाते चलो, क़दम बढ़ाते चलो।।

Gandhian Era
When I think of my past, it reminds me of Gandhian era
Gandhi uplifted the character of each child
He encouraged everyone to get up early, hold the flag of India and go around
Go out with confidence, with peace and love in your heart
Whomsoever you see on the way, hug them and speak to them with love
This is your country, everyone is related to you
Complete your mission, no stopping along the way!

2.2.17 गाँधी की सीख हमें

जीवन हमारा हो खुली पुस्तक, गाँधी ने पाठ सिखाया था।
मन हमारा हो शीशे जैसा, जिसमें कोई काला दाग नहीं।।
व्यवहार हमारा हो ऐसा, छोटे-बड़े सभी का ध्यान बना।
बातें हमारी ऐसी हों, जो सबकी हितकारी हों, मीठी और सुख देने वाली हों।।
ईश्वरीय गुण हैं ये, इनका वरदान मिले सभी को।
प्रार्थना हम सभी की है प्रभु से, ऐसा दो ज्ञान हमें।।

Gandhi Taught us
Gandhi taught us our life should be an open book
Our heart should be as pure as a mirror, there is no dark spot on it
Our behavior should be such
We give proper regard and love to young and old
Our speech and words should be sweet and helpful
So that everyone gets comfort from us
These are divine qualities, we must pray for the grace of God
Oh God! Please grant this knowledge to all.

2.2.18 अग्नि परीक्षा

कोई मेरा कितना भी अपमान करे, नहीं कलुषता आए मन पर।
चेहरा सदा शीतल बना रहे, नहीं अपशब्द मुख से निकलें मेरे।।

तब समझूँगी मुझ में कुछ संयम है, बाक़ी सब व्यर्थ की बातें हैं।
बड़ा सरल उपदेश है देना, पहचान समय पर होती है।।
अग्नि परीक्षा बार-बार होती है, दुर्बलता से मैं दूर रहूँ।
अपने काम में बस लगी रहूँ, स्वस्थ विचार बस बने रहें।।
हाथ जोड़, सिर झुकाए, तेरा आशीर्वाद मुझे प्राप्त रहे। हे ईश!

The Test of a Practical Vedantin

No matter how much someone insults me, I should have no grudge
I must maintain my peace and should not utter impolite words
Only then will I think I have some discipline
It is very easy to give advice, but difficult to follow
We are tested again and again, I pray! God, give me strength!
I wish I have good thoughts all the time and remain busy
With folded hands I bow to you and ask for your blessings.

2.2.19 विनम्रता शृंगार वीर का

सूखा, ठुंठ-वृक्ष एक झटके में धरती पर आ गिरता है।
कच्ची हरी टहनी आँधी तूफ़ानों को सहकर झुकी, विनम्र दिखाई देती है।।
हल्का-फुल्का पक्षी आकाश में ऊँची उड़ान भरता और विचरता है।
देख किसी की नम्रता-कोमलता कमज़ोरी का मत ध्यान करो।।
विनम्रता है शृंगार वीर का, उसका सदैव आदर-सम्मान करो।

Softness a Mark of Strength

It is very easy to cut a dry and old tree
Soft green branches face fierce wind and storm, yet remain strong as they are
Birds fly high, because they are light and strong
Never think they are weak, those who are soft and humble
These are the qualities of the brave and strong
Respect them.

2.2.20 भगवान कहाँ है?

ढूँढा तुझे मन्दिर तीर्थ और गुफ़ाओं में, पुजारी की पूजा में, सभाओं में, व्याख्यानों में।
सन्तोष हुआ नहीं कभी, लगा मन का बहलाव है ये।।
सुबह को जब मज़दूर को देखा, कूड़ा उठाते, झाड़ू लगाते सड़कों पर।
पसीने से लथपथ थी काया, चेहरे पर थी मुस्कान बनी।।

लगा जैसे तू खड़ा दे रहा सांत्वना, देख खून-पसीने को।
यह दृश्य तो दर्शन-प्रेरक था, तू मेरे ह्रदय में ही बैठा था।।
कह रहा था-परिश्रम, दया, प्रेम के बीच हूँ मैं बसा हुआ।

Where is God?

I searched for you in temples, holy places, conferences and lectures
I could not find satisfaction anywhere
In the morning, I saw a laborer removing garbage, cleaning the road
He was handling dirt without proper tools, even then he had a smile on his face
I felt as if God was standing there, looking at his condition, giving him consolation
Inspired by this scene, I heard God's voice from my heart
He was telling me, "I live where people work hard, have kindness and love for each other".

2.2.21 पशुओं पर दया करो

सब जीवों में ईश्वर अंश एक बराबर, सभी को कष्ट बराबर होता है।
मनुष्य बोल रहा है मुख से, उसकी बोली समझ में आती है।।
निरपराध अन्य प्राणी भी बोल रहे हैं, कोई समझ नहीं पाता है।
मारकर उनको जब खाते हैं, यह ध्यान नहीं मन में आता।।
इनकी हत्या है पाप बड़ा, इनको न सताओ। दया करो।।

Be Kind to Animals

All are equal, everybody feels pain, God is present in everybody
The difference is, human beings can speak, people understand them
We are not able to understand other species
When we kill them and eat them, we do not realize their pain
It is a great sin, we must not hurt them, nor kill them. Be kind.

2.2.22 पालतू जानवरों की दशा

माँ! नानी कहानी सुनाती थी, बकरी मैं-मैं करके बोला करती थी।
दिखादो मुझे बकरी को, मैं भी उसको सुनना चाहती हूँ।।
बेटी! मेरे बचपन में-एक बकरा-बकरी दालान में रहते थे।
उनको दाना-चारा रोज़ खिलाते और साथ में खेला करते थे।।

बेटी! अब तो एक अरसे से, वे घरों में नही रहतीं, सब मारकर हैं खाए गए।
फिर भी तू आग्रह करती है तो दिखाउँगी किसी कसाई के खेत पर।।
वहाँ डरे हुए खेत के कोने में, दिखाई दे सकते हैं खड़े हुए।
क्या दुर्दशा हो गई है, घर के पालतू बकरा-बकरी की। बन गए हैं एक कहानी।।

Condition of Pet Animals

Mother, my grandmother used to tell me that goats used to say—'meh meh'
I also want to hear and see that goat
Daughter, in my childhood one male and one female goat used to live in the courtyard
Daily we used to feed them and play with them
Now they do not live in households, people have killed and eaten them
Still if you are interested, I will try to show you on a farm owned by a butcher
They might be standing there in fear, probably you can see them
What a terrible situation has happened to these pet animals - it is a very sad story.

2.2.23 पिंजरे का पंछी

पंछी ने कहा, "सुनो!" एक बहेलिए ने पकड़ मुझे, काटे पंख और एक धनी को बेच दिया।
सोने के पिंजरे में बन्द हुआ और लटकाया गया मुख्य द्वार के निकट मुझे।।
सता-सताकर मुझको शिक्षा दी, मित्रों का मन बहलाया और उनका स्वागत खूब किया।
आँखों में मेरे आँसू थे, हँसकर जीने का अभ्यास किया।।
किसके पास कहाँ मैं जाऊँ। सब खुले आकाश में हैं उड़े हुए।
मेरा क़सूर था, मैं सुन्दर था, योग्यता थी, सहनशीलता थी मुझमें।।
शायद इसलिए सह गया इतनी दुष्टता, अकेलापन और क्रूरता।

Bird in a Cage

Bird said, "A hunter caught me, cut my feathers and sold me to a rich man
He closed me in a golden cage, and hung me near the main door of the house

I was harassed and was taught how to welcome friends, and I did it with great enthusiasm
My eyes were full of tears, I practiced how to smile
I had no choice, all my friends were flying in open air in the sky
My fault was, I was pretty, capable, and had tolerance
Probably because of that I bear so much cruelty, loneliness and crookedness."

2.2.24 सार्थक जीवन

केवल जीने का नाम नहीं है जीवन, नियम-संयम से सबको जीना है।
दुख देख कभी ना हों अधीर, सुख देख कभी ना फूल उठें।।
परिश्रम सें जीवन की बाधा को पार करो, कष्टों को सहर्ष स्वीकार करो।
कायरता पास फटक न सके, अपने बल पर जीवन जी सकें।।
दुखियों से हो सहानुभूति, समय पर उनके आएँ काम।
किसी की भी करें न निन्दा, आदर-प्यार की मन में हो निष्ठा।।
मन में जब कोई शंका हो, महान् पुरुषों का, गीता का सहारा लो।
जीने का सुख तभी मिलेगा, गौरवमय जीवन जीने का।।

Purposeful Life
We must lead a life of discipline, life is not just survival
We should not get nervous to see calamity, nor get ecstatic at receiving good fortune
Accept adverse circumstances calmly, face life's challenges working hard
Have faith in yourself, do not feel weak and helpless
Always be ready to help the needy and the poor
Avoid fault-finding, have respect and love for all
Whenever you have any doubt, consult the Gita and take inspiration from elders
This is the path to happiness and self-respect.

2.2.25 मैं कहाँ रहता हूँ

ढूँढते ढूँढते सब हार गए, मेरा पता किसी को नहीं मिला।
मुझे ढूँढ उन आँखों में, जिनमें करुणा है बरस रही।।
देखो उन चेहरों को, जहाँ प्रेम, सरलता दिखाई देती हो।
हाथ सदा सेवा में हैं लगे हुए, पैर सबके संग हैं बढ़े हुए।।

मैं सदा उनके साथ हूँ रहता, वे मुझको अति प्यारे हैं।

Where to Search God

People tried to find me everywhere, couldn't find me anywhere
Search me in the eyes of those where kindness is reflecting
Look at those faces where love and simplicity is depicting
Where people help each other, work together
God always stays with them; He loves them.

2.2.26 पुरुषार्थ

महान् ग्रन्थों ने धर्म, अर्थ, काम, मोक्ष, चार पुरुषार्थों की ओर ध्यान दिलाया है।
धर्म, अर्थ, काम इसी जीवन में होते हैं, मोक्ष का होना मरणोपरान्त कहा जाता है।।
मोक्ष का किसी को पता नहीं, यह किसी के हाथ की बात नहीं।
'जीवन-मुक्त' समझ में आता है, प्रयत्न से जीवन-काल में ही मुक्ति पाता है।।

Four Values

Our great scriptures have emphasized four duties, dharma, artha, kaam, moksha by human beings
Dharma, artha and kaam are completed in one's life time, moksha is supposed to come after death
Whether one gets moksha or not, nobody knows with certainty
We can only think of Jivan – Mukta, it comes only in this life.

2.2.27 जीवन मुक्त

जीवन्मुक्त संसार के बीच रहकर, मुक्त हुआ है बन्धन से।
सबको अपना सहयोग है देता, नहीं बदले की आशा करता।।
कर्मयोगी होने के कारण, नहीं जाता विरक्ति की ओर।
स्वार्थ पास नहीं फटकता, भला सबका जी जान से चाहता।।
प्रसन्नता चेहरे पर होती, मनो-भावना योगी की, होती।
सबको समान समझता है और प्रिय सभी का होता है।।
जीवन्मुक्त का वर्णन गीता ने किया है, रास्ता छः बार दिखाया है।

Jivan-Mukta (The one who is Liberated)

The liberated one lives in this world but is released from all bonds
She helps everyone without any desire for returns

She is always straightforward, never depressed, and has no desire to escape the world
Being selfless, always eager to help others with her whole heart
Happy to see others happy, working with discipline
Everybody is equal in her eyes, and she is loved by all
The Gita has taught us this, has told us about a Jivan-mukta six times.

2.2.28 विश्वशान्ति का मार्ग-व्यावहारिक वेदान्त

गीतांजली को नोबेल पुरस्कार मिला 1913 में।
तरेसठवें गीत ने संसार को सुनाया -
वेदान्त का संदेश है - हम सब एक हैं।
यूरोप ने संदेश सुना - पर युद्ध की तैयारी की।।
इक्कीसवीं शताब्दी में -
विश्वशान्ति का मार्ग ढूँढने की हो रही है तीव्र चेष्टा।
व्यावहारिक वेदान्त है मानव-जाति के लिए आशा की किरण।।

Practical Vedanta Shows the Way

Some traditions in the world
Discriminated between believers and non-believers
Believers were supposed to go to Heaven, non-believers to Hell
Instead, Vedanta declared emphatically
One-ness of all beings.
Vedanta warned
Separateness will bring disharmony
And cause conflict
We need world peace and harmony
Practical Vedanta shows the way.

2.2.29 पंच शास्त्र

परम्परागत वेदान्त ने पूजा प्रस्थानत्रय को।
ब्रह्मसूत्र, उपनिषद, गीता, को माना वेदान्त का आधार।।
व्यावहारिक वेदान्त ने जगद्-हित की शिक्षा दी।
मोक्ष के बजाय जीवन्मुक्ति को जीवन-लक्ष्य बनाया।।
शान्ति-पर्व और अनुगीता को भी आधार-रूप में अपनाया।
इस प्रकार प्रस्थानत्रय का विस्तार हुआ, पंच-शास्त्र पूजित हुए।।

Panch-Shastra

Traditional Vedanta honored Prasthana-traya,
Made Brahmasutras, Upanishads, Gita, the basis of Vedanta
Practical Vedanta declared jagad-hitam as life's goal,
Emphasized Jivan-Mukti rather than Moksha
Added Shanti-Parva and Anu-Gita as basic texts
So Prasthana-Traya was widened to Panch-Shastra.

2.2.30 रहस्य जीवन का

परम पिता की सन्तान हैं हम, वहीं स्थायी बसेरा है।
धरती है कर्म भूमि हमारी, सेवा के लिए है जन्म लिया।।
पूर्ण-योग से करो कर्म, उत्तर ईश्वर को देना है।
हमारे ऋषियों, मुनियों ने कर त्याग तपस्या, यह रहस्य समझाया है।।
जो कुछ है ज्ञान मिला, उसपर नहीं अधिकार तुम्हारा।
वह तो सबकी पूँजी है, उसे छोड़कर जाना है।।
जब जब धरती पर हेगी चाह हमारी, हम सेवा करने उतरेंगे।
सुचारू रूप से कर, निष्काम कर्म, वापिस फिर घर जाएँगे।।

Nishkam Seva is the Purpose of Life

Gita says—God created mankind along with Yajna.
Yajna teaches—"*idam na mama*"
That is - Man is not the real owner of wealth.
God has given wealth to man,
Saying, use it for the good-of-all.
So Yajna means doing good-to-all,
That is, sacrificing selfishness and greed
And doing Nishkam seva, i.e. selfless service.

2.2.31 सहज-सेवा

संध्या समय, खड़ी बीच बग़ीचे, सोच रही थी खोई-खोई,
कौन-सी बात है, प्रसन्न हूँ इतनी, क्या कोई नई बात हुई।
बारीकी से खोजा कारण, एक निष्कर्ष पर जा पहुँची,
प्रातः समय एक अजनबी आया था, मुग्ध हो गया देख फूल बग़ीचे के।
देख उसके चेहरे की वृत्ति, उठाया फूल का गमला और उसे प्रेम से सौंप दिया,
मुग्ध हुआ उसका मन, आँखें प्रेम से छलछला उठीं।

दिया आशीर्वाद मुझे और स्वयं भाव-विभोर हो चला गया,
बात लगती है छोटी, महत्ता कितनी है सहज देने में।

Highest Sewa is Spontaneous Sewa
Dr. Radhakrishnan interprets Gita Shloka 6.3
To explain the difference between
Duty-bound sewa and spontaneous sewa,
A paid nurse looks after the baby as her duty
She usually works for eight hours a day
The mother looks after her baby naturally and spontaneously
Joyfully she does so for twenty-four hours every day
By God's grace
When I see a poor person
My helping hand is extended spontaneously.

2-2-32 सेवा से सुख-शांति
सुख-शांति हमें नहीं मिलती, हम ढूँढ रहे हैं - मन्दिर, गिरजाघर और गुफ़ाओं में।
वह तो बसी हुई है, हमारे मन-मस्तिष्क, व्यवहार और विचारों में।।
घर के दरवाज़े बंद हुए, भूखे को रोटी दे न सके, जीवन होड़-दिखावे में बीत गया।
देखो उन बच्चों को, पैसे के अभाव में पढ़ न सके, न तन पर कपड़ा है, न सिर पर साया है।।
उसको मिली सुख-शांति, समझा जिसने फूल गुलाब में आदर्श महान्।
वास किया बीच में काँटों के, सुगंध फैलाई चारों ओर, काम आया सदा सभी के।।
श्रद्धा से सब जगह चढ़ाया जाता, औषधि के काम में आता, देख इसे दुःख-दर्द मिटा करते हैं।
जितना खिला, उतना और झुका, नम्रता और सौन्दर्य हर पंखुड़ी में है बसी हुई।।

Sewa is the Way to Peace
How to find peace?
Orthodox priests say - go to the Himalayas, or to temples
Swami Vivekananda said—I have examined the lives of thousands of people

Only those who did Sewa of the poor, get peace.
These people worship daridra-narayana (seeing God in the likeness of the poor)
Be like the rose flower, that lives surrounded by thorns, with fragrance that spreads far
That is used as homage on auspicious occasions, and is soft and gives pleasure the more it blooms
Practical Vedanta interprets karma - yoga thus, as Sewa - yoga.

2.2.33 कौन प्रिय है - व्यावहारिक वेदांत का रूप

दुःख-सुख, शोक-हर्ष, मान-अपमान, सबके जीवन में आते, सभी सहन करते हैं।

वे प्रशंसा के अधिकारी हैं, जो झूठी निन्दा सुनकर भी, बिन बोले, सहर्ष झेला करते हैं।।

विश्वास है परम-पुरुष में, सात्त्विक है वृत्ति, निन्दा-स्तुति से हैं दूर बसे।
समाज-उत्थान की केवल बात हैं करते, निज-स्वार्थ का नामो-निशान नहीं।।
देश के सच्चे सपूत की पहचान यही, कमाई-पूँजी है जीवन की।
न अहंकार है, न कोई दिखावा हैं, ईश्वरीय प्रेरणा से सर्वहित में हैं लगे हुए।।
प्रिय हैं जनता के, मन से हैं शांत, सम्मानित हैं हर दिशा में, हर श्रेणी के लोगों में।

Who are Practical Vedantins?
In Gita, we heard Arjuna's question:
Who is a Sthitaprajna, Gunatita, Bhakta (balanced, worthy, devotee)?
In this book, we ask the question:
Who is a Practical Vedantin?
A Practical Vedantin practices religion that is scientific,
They are un-orthodox, who adjust their practices to time, place, circumstance
They undertake the journey from spirituality to social welfare
And finally to world peace
This is sewa-yoga.

CHAPTER 2.3

Lokasamgraha, Women's Empowerment

(सर्व-हित, महिला गौरव)

2.3.1 लोक-संग्रह

सबके हित की सोच जिसे, अपना हिंत भी उसका निश्चित है।
भगवान ने दे उदाहरण अपना, सबका इस ओर ध्यान किया।।
मुझे नहीं अवकाश मिनटभर, दिनभर काम में हूँ व्यस्त हुआ।
छोड़ दूँ यदि काम एक क्षण, नष्ट समस्त जग हो जाएगा।।
इसी को कहते हैं 'लोक संग्रह' तुम भी 'सर्व हित' का ध्यान रखो।

Good of All

Those who think well of others, they are sure to get their own good
God gave his own example and focused the attention of everybody
He does not take any minute off; the whole day keeps Himself busy
If He leaves work for a second, the whole Universe will collapse
This is called Lokasamgraha, we must always think what is good of others

2.3.2 हितकारी सोच

सर्व-हित की सोच करो, अपना हित है छिपा हुआ।
लेने से पहले देकर देखो, कितना सुख है महसूस हुआ।।
बिन माँगे, बिन आश किए, आगे बढ़कर देखो तुम।
देखोगे चारों ओर मित्र खड़े हैं, आतुर हैं कुछ करने को।।

सुख-शान्ति मिलती तब है, जब "पर-शब्द" हटे मन से।
हम सबके हैं, सब अपने हैं, यह भाव दृढ़ बना रहे।।

Helpful Thinking
Before you think about your own good, wait! First, think!
Think about the welfare of others
Before you accept anything from others, give first to others
You will realize the pleasure from this
First you go forward, without any expectation and without being asked
The result will be, your friends will always be eager to help you
We get peace when we realize we are not separate
We belong to everyone, everyone belongs to us
Remember this.

2.3.3 सच्चा समाज-सेवक

किया अपना और अपने बच्चों का, यह निज कर्त्तव्य हमारा है।
इससे ऊपर उठ, जिसने किया ध्यान समाज का, वह प्रशंसा का अधिकारी है।।
लेना है आसान बहुत, देना जब उससे भी सरल लगे, तभी आदर मिलता है।
व्यक्ति तभी ऊँचा उठता, समाज तरक्की करता, देश आगे बढ़ता है।।
जो सबके लिए करने को तैयार, वह ऋणी नहीं, त्यागी कहलाता है।

Real Servant of Society
Whatever we do for ourselves and for our children, that is our personal duty
Who go beyond their own people and serve the society
They get higher respect from all around
Those people get bigger honor who get more pleasure in giving rather than taking
With such actions, one uplifts oneself, society becomes strong and country is admired
Those who are ready to work for all, they repay their debt to society
They are the pillars of society.

2.3.4 सभी सभ्य हैं

सभी स्वयं को सभ्य बोलते, चाहे किसी देश के वासी हों।

समाज सभ्य उसी को कहता जो सबको समान समझ सत्कार करे।।
ऊँच-नीच का ध्यान नहीं, मर्यादा का ना किया उल्लंघन, समय पर सबके आया काम।
जी-जान से छोटों को प्यार किया, बड़ों को न पहुँचाई ठेस कभी।।
हर देश की मर्यादा भिन्न बनी, उसी के अनुसार स्वयं को ढाल लिया।
प्रशंसा में किसी की करे न कमी कभी, सब के हित की चाह करे।।
ऐसी सोच सभी को प्रिय बनाती, चाहे किसी देश के वासी हों।

Everyone Thinks I am Cultured

Everyone calls themselves cultured, no matter which country one belongs to,
Society calls cultured to those only who respect everyone equally
They do not think who is rich, who is poor, never cross the norms and always ready to help at the right time
They love youngsters at heart, never hurt elders
Of course in every country principles are different, but they adjust accordingly
They are never miserly in appreciating others and always think good of others
This type of thinking makes a person very dear, no matter which country one belongs to

2.3.5 नारी सबला है

सबला को अबला की मिले उपाधि, यह नारी को मंजूर नहीं।
पाल-पोसकर बच्चे बड़े है करती, हाथ से काम को नहीं छोड़ती।।
जीवन के हर मोड़ पर भाई, पिता और पति की बनी है शक्ति।
देश पर जब संकट आए, ले तलवार हाथ में, वीरता का सबक़ सिखाया।।
सीता ने राम का साथ दिया, जंगल-जंगल घूमी, अंत में आश्रम में प्रस्थान किया।
शकुन्तला, सावित्री जैसी नारी जहाँ हैं जन्मीं, वहाँ नारी सदा सबला है।
अबला कहकर नारी का मत अपमान करो, सच को सच ही रहने दो।।

Woman is Capable

Woman is not ready to accept that she is weak, surely she is capable

She raises children doing hard work, never leaves work in hand
All the time in difficulty, she helps everybody, she is a big strength for father and husband
At the time of any kind of danger in the country, she is ready to fight and wants to prove her strength
Sita continuously faced all the calamities in jungles, and in the end, with no fault of hers, lived in an ashram
India produced women like Shakuntala and Savitri, how can anybody say woman is weak
It is an insult to her if anybody says she is weak, there is no truth in it

2.3.6 जनक-पत्नी की शिक्षा

कर्म बने पूजा मेरी, सर्व-हित बने धर्म मेरा।
सब प्राणी में दीखे सूरत तेरी, दरिद्रों में हो ध्यान मेरा।।
सेवा-प्रेरक जनक-पत्नी ने उच्च स्वर में कहा, "सुनो!
महिला-गौरव अनुगीता में, जगत् में हो इसका प्रचार"।।

Teaching of Janak's Wife

May my work be my worship, may Lokasamgraha be my faith
May I see God in all beings, particularly in the poor and vulnerable
Janak's wife gave this teaching with strong emphasis
As our scripture Anu-Gita emphasizes women's pride, so may this be adopted throughout the world
This is the second time we admire Janak's wife, from a new angle.

2.3.7 लोक संग्रह बीज-मंत्र

इक्कीसवीं सदी का मंत्र लोक-संग्रह, सबको संग्रहित करने का।
बीज-मंत्र है, आपस की फूट, लड़ाई-झगड़े, सबको रोकने का।।
पढ़ाई-लिखाई और साइंस ने बड़े चमत्कार किए, लड़ाई और बैर को ना रोक सके।
ऊपर से बने बड़े हैं ज्ञानी, भीतर का खोखलापन ना देख सके।।
शांति स्थापित होगी तब, जब भाईचारा, प्रेम सरलता, सहनशीलता व्यवहार में आएगी।

समस्त गुणों का निचोड़ लोक-संग्रह, एक दिन दुनिया अपनाएगी।।

Main Message of the 21st Century

Good of all is the main message of the 21st Century, it unites
It is the key point to stop war and all enmity
We are very much advanced in science and education, but could not stop wars
We look very intelligent and knowledgeable, but problems are beyond our reach
We can achieve peace only when we follow the way of peace through brotherhood, love and tolerance
Good of all is the essence of all the qualities, and we are sure people will invariably follow it in the future.

2.3.8 सर्व हित की इच्छा वाला

'सर्व हित' की इच्छा वाला, स्वयम् को सुखी बनाता है।
सभी उससे प्रेम हैं करते, सबको शान्ति पहुँचाता है।।
स्वार्थ, झूठ, चालाकी नहीं पास फटकती, सरल-हृदय होता है।
चेहरा बना शान्त, आँखों में दया दिखाई देती है।।
सदा सभी का सहायक, देख सभी को हर्षित होता है।
उसपर ईश्वर की कृपा निराली, चारों ओर से सम्मानित होता है।।

One Who Desires Good of All

One who desires good of all becomes happy herself
Everyone loves her and she gives peace to everyone
Selfishness, lies, and cunningness never touch her and she is always gentle at heart
Her face is always calm and kindness reflects in her eyes
She will always be helpful and happy to see others happy
She gets special blessings from God and receives honor everywhere

2.3.9 अन्तर्यामी

देख हृदय की व्याकुलता, अन्तर्यामी मुझसे बोल उठा।
सरल, स्वच्छ और निर्मल रख अपने मन को, दुर्बलता का नाम न ले।।
सीधी-सच्ची बात करो, हेर-फेर की ना सोच रखो।
सुख-शान्ति हर पल साथ चलेगी, मेरे ऊपर विश्वास करो।।

'सर्व-हित परहित' में लगे रहो, निर्णय सब मुझपर छोड़ो।
चिंता न कर किसी बात की, मैं सबके मन का ज्ञाता हूँ।।

God is Inside

Seeing the pain in my heart, God, sitting inside me, taught
Keep your heart and mind pure, simple and strong
Do not bring any weakness into your heart
Speak with a pure heart, don't twist the reality
Have confidence in yourself, peace will reflect on your face
Keep yourself busy in helping others, decision should be left to Me
And don't worry. I know your inner thoughts.

2.3.10 सब कुछ अन्दर है

देख सभी का चेहरा, जिसका चेहरा खिल उठा।
देख किसी व्याकुल को, जिसका मन मुरझा गया।।
घायल की गति को वह ही जान सका।
जिसने अपने को उसमें झाँका हो।।
वह ही हर्षित है, वह ही सुखी है।
जहाँ अपना-पराया मन से निकल गया।।
जिसकी ऐसी हो भावना मन में।
उसे बाहर ढूँढने से क्या कुछ मिला कभी।।

Be Happy to See Everyone

Be happy to see everyone
Get concerned seeing the sadness of someone
Only they can realize the pain of others, who think everyone alike
They are the happy ones who never think of anybody as alien
Or see others differently from oneself
They are the ones who find peace inside.

2.3.11 एक पिता की संतान हैं हम

खोई-खोई, अकेले, एकान्त में झरने के निकट थी खड़ी हुई।
देख उसे लगी पूछने, तू इतना प्रसन्न क्यूँ है? इस एकाकीपन में।।
कल कल की आई आवाज़, खोल डाला सारा रहस्य जीवन का मुझे समझाने को।

तेरा, मेरा उद्गम स्थान एक है, एक दिशा से, वापिस लौटकर जाते हैं।।
हर समय व्यस्त हूँ, जूझ रहा हूँ, चट्टानों से, बड़े बड़े वृक्षों से, आँधी तूफ़ानों से।
डरता नहीं, कोई नहीं शत्रु मेरा, सबने आगे बढ़ने का सबक़ सिखाया।।
गाता हूँ, प्रसन्न रहता हूँ, अपने संग सबको लेकर चलता हूँ।
साफ़-सुथरा हूँ, सहायक हैं ये रोड़े पत्थर, ये सब हैं मित्र मेरे।।
सबक़ सीख ले मेरे से, एक ही पिता की सन्तान हैं हम। आगे बढ़।

We are All Children of God

I was lost and standing near a brook
Astonished to see why it was so happy being alone
As if it was telling me something about the reality of life
Both of us are coming from the same source and we will return to the same
I am continuously busy, struggling with rocks, huge trees and heavy storms
They taught me fearlessness, I have no enemy and I have learnt how to continuously move forward
In spite of all the difficulties, I sing, I remain happy and keep moving on
Storms are my companions, helping me stay strong and fresh
Learn a lesson of life from me. We come from the same source!

2.3.12 भगवान् का प्यारा कौन?

कमल भगवान् की शय्या है, कीचड़ में है जन्म हुआ।
गुलाब गले का हार बना, काँटों में है पला हुआ।।
जितने जिसने कष्ट उठाए, उतने ही वे निखरे हैं।
भगवान् को वे हैं अति प्यारे, सबके वे बने सहारे हैं।।
जिसने यह बात समझ ली है, उसने सहर्ष कठिनता को पार किया।

Who is Dear to God?

God chose lotus as his bed because dirt is its origin
Rose is God's garland because it grows in the company of thorns
In reality, those who suffer more, they groom better
Such people always help others a lot, so they become dear to God

Those who understand this theory, they cross difficulties of life easily

2.3.13 विनती है मेरी

विनती है मेरी, सबका किया सदा याद रहे।
अपने किए का मन पर बोझ न हो।।
समझ सभी के हित को अपना।
करूँ निशदिन अपना काम।।
मन में किसी तरह का अभिमान न हो।
अपने पराए का कोई ध्यान नहीं।।
देख सफलता हर प्राणी की।
खुशी से मन मेरा फूल उठे।।
आशीर्वाद मिले सदा तेरा।
मेरा उत्साह सदा बना रहे।।

This is My Prayer

I should always remember what others have done for me
We should not dwell on what we do for others
Let me gain satisfaction from working day and night for the good of others
I should never feel arrogance; nor difference between mine and thine
The success of others should bring me joy
God! Grant me such enthusiasm for the service of others
My resolve may always be thus maintained

2.3.14 मुस्कान बनूँ

मुस्कान बनूँ उन चेहरों की, जिनका हृदय देख मुझे खुशी से फूल उठे।
पीड़ित के दर्द को दूर करूँ, दुखिया के आँसू पोंछ सकूँ।।
बैठ अकेला, घर के कोने में, राह कोई जब तकता हो।
जाकर वहाँ मैं बैठ सकूँ, धीरज, सान्त्वना के दो शब्द कह सकूँ।।
समझूँगी मेरा जीवन सफल हुआ, मैंने भी गीता से कुछ सीखा है।

I Want to Give Happiness to All

I want to be the cause of happiness for all whom I meet

I want to remove the pain of others, and wipe the tears of people in distress
I like to sit with a person who is alone, and say a few words of consolation and peace
If I am able to do all this
Only then I will think I have learnt the Gita.

2.3.15 जिसका है उसे लौटाना है

ख़ाली हाथ थे आए, ख़ाली हाथ ही जाना है, कहावत सदा सुनते आए।
इसका संबंध संसार से है, जिससे मिला उसी को देना है।।
भगवान से जो कुछ मिला, साथ ही लाए साथ ही ले जाएँगे।
कहाँ से है यह कला मिली, कहाँ से है संगीत मिला।।
कहाँ से है बुद्धि मिली, कहाँ से है यह प्रेम-भाव मिला।
प्रेरणा सब मिली उसी से, संसार में कुछ करने को।।
यह ईश्वर का वायदा है, जितना इसका प्रयोग किया, उतना ही और मिला।
उसी की है, उसी को उत्तर देना है, प्रयोग के लिए है हमें मिली।
समय तेज़ी से है ढल रहा, भूल न कहीं हम से हो जाए।।

What We Take We Have to Return

We came empty handed, we will go empty handed
We always heard
Whatever we get in this world, we have to return with thanks
God sent us with special faculties, we use them for social benefit
Some are exceptionally intelligent, some are very emotional and considerate
Inspiration we get from Him to share the burden of life and help each other
Whatever we do, God encourages
We are answerable to Him
How we used God-given gifts for the good of all.

2.3.16 दायित्व

छोटे, बड़े, नाती, पोते, संगी, साथी और पड़ोसी, सभी समाज का हिस्सा हैं।
सहायता और प्रभाव से सबके, हम आगे बढ़ते हैं, जीवन चलता है।।
इनके रहो सदा आभारी, जीवन में सुख मिलता है।

सबका उपकार बहुत है हमपर, हमारा भी है दायित्व बना।।
समय कहीं चूक न जाए, यथा समय अपना कर्ज़ चुकाओ।

Social Responsibility
Youngsters, elders, grand children, friends and neighbours
All are part of the society
With the help and influence of all we go ahead and succeed in life
We should always be grateful to them, it gives peace and purpose in life
Their contribution is very high, we should recognize our responsibility
Before it is too late, we must fulfill our duties and repay the debt.

2.3.17 पर-हित की महत्ता

दया, धर्म, ध्यान और पूजा, या फिर हो विद्वत्ता।
तीर्थ, पुण्य, जाप करो, या बड़े बड़े व्याख्यान करो।।
सबका महत्त्व तभी है ऊँचा, परहित का हो ध्यान बना।
अनुगीता ने यह पाठ सिखाया, जो है पढ़ने योग्य सर्वैः।।

Think of Others First
Kindness, duty, meditation, prayer, learning, or visiting holy places
Doing religious acts or giving big lectures;
They are all good only when we think about others
Anu Gita emphasized this; and so we should all read it.

2.3.18 अतिथि

बिना सूचना के घर जो आया, उसे अतिथि कहते हैं।
उसका करो आदर-सम्मान सदा, घर में जगह की कोई कमी नहीं।।
मन छोटे होते हैं, भोजन स्थान से हैं घर भरे हुए।
जहाँ सभी सम्मानित होते, समझो हँसी, खुशी से है घर भरा हुआ।।
मानसिक रोग और अकेलापन, छू सका क्या उन्हें कभी?
गुरु जनों की सीख यही थी, ध्यान में रखें हम सभी।

Guest
In reality a guest is one, who comes without prior information

There is no shortage of space in the house, we should always welcome them
People are small minded, the house is full of food and is big enough
Those who respect everyone, they are the happy and cheerful ones
Rarely they feel loneliness, hardly they get mental sickness
Our elders gave this teaching.
Keep it in your mind.

CHAPTER 2.4

Daridra - Narayana - Seeing the Poor as the Image of God

दरिद्रनारायण

2.4.1 दरिद्रनारायण

दरिद्रनारायण का संदेश ऋषियों ने दिया हमें।
स्वामी विवेकानन्द ने इस शब्द का निर्माण किया।।
टैगोर ने गीतांजली के दसवें और ग्यारहवें गीतों में सुनाया विश्व को।
हे भगवन्! हम तुझे मंदिरों में रहे ढूँढते।।
अब हम समझे हैं कि तू तो उन दरिद्रों के बीच में है।
जो भूखे-प्यासे, धूप में, परिश्रम करते हुए, पसीने में लथपथ हैं।।

God is Among the Poorest
Rishis gave us the message of Daridra-Narayana
Swami Vivekananda coined this eye-opening expression
Tagore's Gitanjali, in the tenth and eleventh hymns
Declared to the world, through two scriptural songs
Open thine eyes, and see
Thy God is not in this lonely dark corner of the temple
But walks in the clothes of the humble among the poorest, lowliest and lost souls
Who toil under the heat of the burning sun, covered in sweat.

2.4.2 दरिद्र-सेवा के आदर्श

बुद्ध छोड़ राजमहल, हो गए लीन जन सेवा में
गांधी ने जानबूझकर अपनाई दरिद्रता और रहे भंगी बस्ती में।।
खाते-पीते घर छोड़ विवेकानन्द, दर दर घूमे और ज्ञान का संदेश दिया।

नेहरू ने दे दिया अपना घर महल-सा, और देश के लिये दे दिये गहने पत्नी के।।
इन सबका था त्याग बड़ा, सभी का ध्यान ग़रीब की सेवा और देश प्रेम में था लगा हुआ।
सराहनीय है ऐसे महापुरुषों का जीवन, जो समान समझ सबकी सेवा में हैं लगे हुए।।

Inspiring Ideals of Service to the Poor
Buddha gave up his palace to serve mankind
Gandhi identified himself as one of the poor and stayed in scavenger's colony
Vivekananda walked thousands of miles to help the poor
Nehru donated his big house to Congress, and even sold his wife's ornaments to serve the country
Millions have been inspired by these examples
To serve the poor, seeing God in them.

2.4.3 दरिद्र-प्रेमी नारियाँ

पुरातन युग में अमर हुई सावित्री, करी धनहीन सास-ससुर की सेवा।
आधुनिक समय में मीराबेन, निवेदिता और मदर थरेसा ने करी ग़रीबों में सेवा।।
अमर हो गया इनका नाम, देश छोड़ अपना, त्यागी हो गई दरिद्रों की सेवा में।
संसार पूजता है इनको, और भारत गौरव से इनका नाम है लेता।।

Women Holding up Service for the Poor
Savitri became famous, not as a princess
But as a daughter-in-law who uplifted her parents-in-law to prosperity
Nivedita came from the West, to serve the poor in India
Miraben also came from the West, as a disciple of Gandhi, to serve the poor
Mother Theresa picked up abandoned children and made them her family members
Such examples glorify women who consider the poor as their own children.

2.4.4 शबरी के बेर

दो सूखे प्रेम से खाए शबरी के बेर, राम का हृदय पुलकित हो उठा।

पाकर सुदामा के मुट्ठी-भर तंदुल, कृष्ण ने सुदामा को गले लगाया।।
भगवान् प्रसन्न नहीं होते शान-शौक़त और झूठे दिखावे से।
ईश्वर को वे लगते हैं प्यारे जो सीधे-सादे, धन-हीन, कर्त्तव्य परायण हैं।।
कभी न भूलो अपने दरिद्र मित्र, ग़रीब पड़ौसी को, देखो सत्यता उनमें।
भगवान् की होती उनपर कृपा निरन्तर, जो सबको समान समझते हैं।।

Remember Shabri and Sudama
Shabri, the poor old woman, became worthy of Ram's love
The pre-tasted berries that she offered
Were received by Rama as the most delicious
Sudama walked without shoes to Dwarka
He offered Tandul, the poor men's rice, and that too just a little packet wrapped in a worn-out piece of cloth
Krishna embraced him and uplifted him from poverty to prosperity
Follow whole - heartedly what modern Rishi's have taught
"Serve the poor, seeing God in them."

2.4.5 दरिद्र-सेवा ही ईश्वर सेवा

विवेकानन्द ने सभी वर्ग के लोगों की करी है सेवा।
दरिद्र को तो नारायण का ही रूप दिया।।
दरिद्र है समाज का ऐसा अंग।
जो सरल है, सहज है, और करता है अधिक परिश्रम।।
धनी वर्ग उसका करता है शोषण।
यह समाज सेवा के अनुकूल नहीं।।
देख समाज में उनकी व्यथित दशा।
विवेकानन्द ने उनकी करी है सेवा।।
माना इसको ईश्वर सेवा।
समाज में नया उदाहरण बना दिया।।

To Serve the Poor Means to Serve God
Vivekananda walked thousands of miles
Helping all those who needed help
People asked him, "How to worship God?"
He told them, "By helping the poor,"

"Why are they poor?" People asked him
"Is it because they committed sin in their previous life?"
Vivekananda said, "No. This is a wrong excuse.
Rich people have exploited them.
Their children did not receive education
So poverty continued from generation to generation
God does not approve such exploitation
So God will be happy if we end exploitation of the poor."

2.4.6 दरिद्र-सेवक

मन हुआ बेचैन, देखी जाड़े से ठिठुरती हुई एक भिखारिन।
उतार तन से कपड़ा अपना, उढ़ा दिया और किया उसका कष्ट निवारण।।
भूखे को जब मिली न रोटी, अपना आधा भोजन उसको सौंप दिया।
एक निर्धन का बच्चा पढ़ने की इच्छा रखता था, अभाव था पैसे का।।
हाथ में उसके जो था पैसा, तुरन्त उसके हाथ में सौंप दिया।
धन्य है ऐसे व्यक्ति का जीवन, देख व्यथा निःसहाय व्यक्ति की।।
भूल गया सब स्वार्थ अपना, रो पड़ा देख दशा व्यथित की।
सच्चे शब्दों में कहलाया सेवक बन गया अपने में एक उदाहरण।।

Those Who Serve God by Serving the Poor
Helping those that can not help themselves
Giving one's own clothing or shelter to those that have none
Sharing food with the hungry
Extending your helping hand to help the children of the poor to educate
Blessings will come to such people
Who feel others' pain as if it were their own
They are the examples to humankind

2.4.7 हितकारी कौन है?

'पर-पीड़ा' से जो द्रवित नहीं, 'परहित' के सुख को क्या जाने।
दीन बच्चों की सेवा कर न सका, वह वात्सल्य सुख को क्या समझा।।
दुखिया के आँसू पोंछ न सका, करुण-रस को क्या जान सका।
अपना हित रख सबसे पीछे, जो सबके आया काम सदा।।
वह ही सच्चा सेवक है, वह ही सबका 'हितकारी' है।

Who Helps the Poor?

Those who do not understand the pain of others, how can they rejoice in other people's pleasure
Those who cannot serve poor and weak children, how can they understand what filial love is
Those who cannot wipe the tears of an old woman, how can they know what distress is
The really helpful person is he who always keeps the welfare of others first
And thinks about himself the last.

2.4.8 दरिद्र-प्रेमी

प्रेमी वह है जिसने सुनी सबकी करुण पुकार।
दरिद्रों की करी है सेवा, अपाहिज को सदा दिया सहारा।।
पीड़ित के आँसू पोंछे, किसी अकेले के पास है जाकर बैठा।
कभी गुमान नहीं करने का, सदा सभी का साथ निभाया।।
अपने समान समझ सभी को, सबके काम में हाथ बँटाया।

Loving Person

One who hears the pathetic voice of others, is called a loving person
He serves the poor and always helps the disabled
Goes and gives solace to those who are crying with pain
Has no arrogance and is always ready to help
Considers himself equal to everyone and tries his best to share in their hardships.

2.4.9 दान नहीं, सेवा है उत्तम

दान देकर मत समझो फ़र्ज़ पूर्णतः सेवा का है चुका दिया
सब किसी के पास नहीं है पैसा, हैं असमर्थ देने में।।
कभी अहंकार भी देखा जाता है देने में दान।
इसके विपरीत सेवा भाव से किया कर्म बड़ा सात्त्विक कहलाता है।।
इसमें दिखाई देती है नम्रता, शीतलता, प्यार और त्याग।
अहंकार नहीं है करने में, प्रसन्नता हृदय में है भरी हुई।।
अपने समान, सभी का है सम्मान किया।

Not Charity, Service is Better

Traditional Vedanta advised people to give charity to the poor
Practical Vedanta says that charity often implies pity
Modern thinkers insist that help to the poor
Should be considered their rightful claim
Help the poor through Sewa (or service)
Sewa should be selfless, free from arrogance and pity.

2.4.10 तिरस्कार

कोई जगह नहीं है तेरी, किसी पर तेरा अधिकार नहीं।
छोड़ दे घमंड अपनेपन का, यह सीधा-सच्चा मार्ग नहीं।।
मत ललकारना कभी किसी को, समझ उसे अपने से छोटा।
सोच सदा अपने मन में, मैं बैठा हूँ निर्धन की कुटिया में।।
एक तरह से सबको देख रहा, तिरस्कार का कभी नाम न ले।
जो मुझको सब में देख रहा, उनके सदा निकट हूँ मैं।।
वे प्रतिक्षण मुझको भजते हैं, मैं जी जान से उनको चाहता हूँ।

Haughtiness

It is not right to be haughty, it leads to difficulties
Never scold anybody, thinking yourself great
Realize, the poor and the down-trodden are very dear to God
Treat them with due respect
God is close to those who treat all equally with love
They serve God and He loves them dearly.

2.4.11 प्रसन्नता

प्रसन्नता कहती है—मत ढूँढो मुझको गहनों में, कपड़ों में, चलचित्रों में, भोजनालयों में।
मैं इतनी सस्ती नहीं हूँ, मैं सरलता में, सादगी में, अतिथि सेवा में, भूखे को भोजन देने में।।
प्रेम से करो सबसे बातें, अमीर ग़रीब में कोई भेद नहीं।
काम सभी के आओ निरन्तर, करो जी जान से सेवा सबकी।।
तिरस्कार की भावना नहीं हो मन में, प्यार, आदर भरे हों मन में।
जहाँ होगा साम्राज्य इनका, प्रसन्नता वहाँ दिखाई देगी सबको।।
मैं ढूँढने की वस्तु नहीं, सेवा-भाव अपनाओ।

Happiness

I am not somewhere outside—do not try to find me in luxuries of life
You can not find me in ornaments, in expensive clothes, cinema houses or in restaurants
Look for me inside, I live in simplicity, feeding the hungry and in serving the poor
Talk politely without having distinction between rich and poor
Serve everyone whole heartedly and continuously
Keep love and kindness in your heart, never let down anybody
Where these qualities exist, happiness will be there
So find me in Sewa and not in luxurious enjoyments.

CHAPTER 2.5

Karma Adjusted to Time, Place and Circumstance

(कर्म योग, देश-काल-पात्र)

2.5.1 समयानुसार कर्म करो

धर्म परिस्थिति और समयानुसार अदलता-बदलता रहता है।
ज्ञान, भक्ति और कर्म देश-काल-रूप ही चलते हैं।।
जिस समय जैसी आवश्यकता आन पड़े, उसी के अनुसार कर्म करो।
व्यावहारिक वेदान्त में अनिवार्य होता कर्मयोग।।
निःस्वार्थ भाव से काम जो करते, ईश्वर उनका साथ है देता।।
साहस और हिम्मत आती है, कार्य सफल हो जाते हैं।।
समय की पुकार सुनो, काम में सदा जुटे रहो।

Action Should Be at the Right Moment
Actions change according to time and place
Knowledge, faith, and actions all depend upon time
We should act according to the need of the time
Practical Vedanta puts Karmayoga in the front
Those who have faith and work attentively, having no selfish motive, they get help from God
They become strong and brave and get success in action
Think about the need of the time and go on doing your duty

2.5.2 अधिकार

अधिकार, अधिकार की बातें करते, क्या अधिकार हुआ कभी किसी का।
जो अधिकार को छोड़ चला, उसको सारे अधिकार मिले।।
ख़ाली हाथ आए थे, ख़ाली हाथ चले जाएँगे, सोच इसकी क्यों करते हैं।

कर्त्तव्य पर है केवल अधिकार हमारा, यही सबसे बड़ा अधिकार हमारा।।
ऐसी सोच जहाँ होती है, दुःख दूर भगा करते हैं।
याद करो गीता का सन्देश।।

Only Right to Work
Nobody gets rights by talking about it all the time
One who does not emphasize claim on rights gets the reward
We should not worry about rights, we came with empty hands and we are going to part with empty hands
We get all the rights when we care only for our actions and duties
When we think in that direction, all our sorrows disappear
This is the teaching of Gita (Shloka 2.47)

2.5.3 सन्तुलित मार्ग
अधिकारों को भूल जाओ, अपने करे का कभी रखो न ध्यान।
यह शिक्षा माँ से सीखो, पालती-पोसती योग्य बनाती।।
रात-रात जगती, निष्काम-भाव से काम है करती।
बालक बड़ा हुआ, लगा कमाने, नए व्यक्ति जीवन में आए।।
सभी पुराना नहीं ग़लत, सभी नया नहीं सही।
दोनो में रखो सन्तुलन और आगे बढ़ने की ओर चलो।।

Balanced Way of Life
Do not think about your rights, never regard yourself as the doer
Learn this from mothers who raise their children and make them capable
She keeps herself awake the whole night and works selflessly
Child grows up, starts earning, new people come in life
Completely forget their childhood, it becomes like a dream
All their childhood learning is not bad, nor every learning afterwards is good
Proceed further, but keep balance between the two.

2.5.4 तीन प्रकार के व्यक्ति
तीन प्रकार के व्यक्तियों से समाज है रचा हुआ।
प्रत्येक व्यक्ति में सात्त्विक, राजसी, तामसिक तीनों गुण कुछ मात्रा में दिखाई देते हैं।।

कर्मानुसार एक सात्त्विक, एक राजसी और एक तामसिक कहलाता है।
सात्त्विक करता धर्म का आचरण, निष्कपट, निश्छल, निष्कामी होता है।।
स्वयं नहीं उत्तेजित होता और सभी को शीतलता देता है।
राजसी आम व्यक्ति होते, दुःख-सुख के भागी होते, कभी शांत तो कभी उत्तेजित होते हैं।।
तामसिक कठोर हृदय वाला, कपटी, सबको पीड़ित करता है।
हर व्यक्ति प्रयत्न शील होने पर तामसिक से राजसी होता हुआ सात्त्विक बन सकता है।।

Three Types of Persons
Gita has classified persons in three categories
Sattvika, Rajasi, and Tamasik
Although all three Gunas (categories) exist in every human being
Tamasika persons look after selfish interests only
Rajasi persons look after their families only
Sattvika persons work for the good-of-all
Of course, this movement upward is possible, if one tries
So Tamasika persons should try to become Rajasi, and then Sattvika.

2.5.5 कर्त्तव्य पूर्ण करो

धरती पर रहते हैं, ब्रह्मन् से साँसों की डोरी से हैं जुड़े हुए।
एक छोर हमसे है जुड़ा हुआ, दूजा ब्रह्मन् के हाथों टिका हुआ।।
प्रेरणा ईश्वर से मिल रही, हम लगे हुए हैं सहज निज-कर्मों के करने में।
समय थोड़ा है, हाथ से निकल न जाय, सहायक खड़े हैं चारों ओर।।
कर्त्तव्य अपना जल्दी-जल्दी कर डालो, लेने-देने में संतुलन बना रहे।
स्वार्थ-रहित सेवा ही है धर्म हमारा, कर्म ही प्रभु की पूजा है।।

Fulfill Your Duties
We live on earth and are connected with God through our breath
One end we are holding and the other end is in the hands of God
Getting inspiration from Him, we are busy in our daily affairs
We must realize that time moves very fast, no matter how much help we get from others

We must never fail in our duty, and should keep balance between what we get and what we give
Selfless action is our duty and motto, and our prayer to God.

2.5.6 कल पर काम न छोड़ो

कल-कल की जब बात करी, समय हाथ से निकल गया।
समय क्या कभी लौटकर आया? अभी काम का आरम्भ करो।।
आरम्भ है अति कठिन, अन्त में मीठे-फल मिलते हैं।
मन से, शुभ कामना लेकर, संग लेकर सबका, जुटे रहो।।
काम अधूरे कभी नहीं रहेंगे, आरम्भ आज ही करके देखो।

Do not Leave Your Work for Tomorrow

Time goes out of our hand, when we go on postponing
Time does not come back, start the work right now
Starting is always difficult, but the results are always sweet
The clue is—have good thoughts and feelings
Join hands with everyone and march on
Do right now, nothing will remain incomplete.

2.5.7 कल और आज

कल की ना बात करो, आनेवाले कल पर ना ध्यान धरो।
आज अभी सब कर डालो, फिर उसको भी जाओ भूल।।
कल शब्द दुखी बनाता है, असमंजस में हमें डालता है।
ध्यान वर्तमान का सुखी बनाता है, सारी विपदा दूर भगाता है।।
सुख-दुख तराज़ू के पलड़े हैं, ऊँचे-नीचे होते रहते हैं।

Past and Present

Do not brood over the past, nor worry about the future
Do your work right now, and forget it afterwards
Postponing makes you unhappy and brings confusion
We get peace when we think only of present, and stay away from old problems
To achieve success, read the famous book entitled "Now".

2.5.8 वरदान दो

ऐसा दो वरदान मुझे—बीते दिन की ना याद करूँ, आगे की मन में सोच न हो।
लगा आज पर ध्यान सदा, अपने पर विश्वास करूँ।।

जितना जिसका संग मिला, उसे सोच मैं प्रसन्न रहूँ।
समय हमारे हाथ नहीं, व्यर्थ की बात में समय गँवाऊँ नहीं।।
एक पग का है पता मुझे, दूसरे पग का ज्ञान नहीं।
ना करूँ किसी बात की चिन्ता, बस चलती रहूँ, चलती रहूँ।।

Give me Your Blessing

I should not think of the past, think what I have to do now; God bless me thus
I must have confidence in myself, and think only about my present action
I should always be happy, whatever time I got to spend with someone
I have no control over time, I should not waste it
I do not know what is going to happen now, how can I talk of the future
I should not worry at all, must keep myself busy in going ahead

2.5.9 दोनों जगत का नाता गहरा

स्थूल जगत् और सूक्ष्म जगत् का नाता गहरा, हम सब उसी से हैं जुड़े हुए।
आवागमन बस होता रहता, एक पिता की सन्तान हैं सब।।
अंत समय में प्रियजनों ने, मित्रों ने, कैसे किया सत्कार और क्या कह कर दी विदाई।
यही हमारी जमा पूँजी, और कमाई है, बस यही छोड़कर हम जाते हैं।।
अन्यथा ख़ाली हाथ आए थे, खुले हाथों ही फिर चले गए।
सदैव हमारा ध्यान इस ओर रहे, सभी रूप से सत्कर्म में लगे रहें।।

Link between Inner and Outer Worlds

Inner and outer worlds are deeply connected, so we are all inter-linked
All of us come and go but source is one
In the end how our friends and relatives depart us, that is our real wealth
This is what we will leave behind – otherwise we came with empty hands and we will leave also the same way
This should always be kept in mind, remembering these thoughts keep busy in good deeds.

2.5.10 काल-चक्र

चौरासी वर्ष के दीर्घ काल में, हर बात बदलती देखी है।
ब्रिटिश-साम्राज्य का तख़्ता पलट गया, देशों की सीमा बदल गई।।
साइंस ने की है तरक़्क़ी, दूरी का आभास नहीं।
अब मोटर गाड़ी की चाल है धीमी लगती, माइक्रोवेव गरम करता देरी से।।
क्षण भर में दुनिया के कोने-कोने से, वार्तालाप सभी का होता।
पैसे का है बोल बाला, दुनिया के चक्कर खूब हैं लगते।।
खुशियाँ तो तब भी थीं, भरी दोपहरी में आँगन के बीच बैठ।
गन्ने चूसते, सिंघाड़े खाते, गपशप करते, धाई मिचौनी खेला करते थे।।
अकेलेपन का जुबान पर नाम नहीं था, डिमैंशिया का किसी को पता नहीं था।
अन्दर कुछ, बाहर कुछ, ऐसी बातों का तो ज्ञान न था, चारों ओर सरलता थी।।
कौन-सा समय है अच्छा, समझ से परे की बात बनी।
चलने का नाम है ज़िन्दगी, रुकने का नाम है मौत, यही समझ में आता है।।

Wheel of Time

I saw evrything changing in eighty-four years of my life
British rulers have gone; boundaries of many countries have changed
Science has become so advanced, we have forgotten the concept of distance
Do not appreciate how fast the motor runs, even we say microwave heats slowly
In a minute we contact different parts of the world; in every part of the world there is no shortage of money
Do we realize we were happy even before the advancement of science
There was no Alzheimer's or dementia; we had no idea of loneliness
People were simple at heart, no showing off
We are not able to see if we are better off today or better off in the past
After realization I feel—go on, go on—this is the way of life.

2.5.11 किश्ती

जीवन एक किश्ती है, जो संसार सागर में है तैर रही।

कारीगर ने ऐसी बनाई, जिसमें नहीं कलुषता, नहीं बोझ, सीधे-सादे ढंग से चलती है।।
नहीं कोई बाधा ऐसी जो इसको रोक सके, इसका ध्येय है चलने का।
मार्ग में चाहे जितने रोड़े-पत्थर हों, या बड़े पेड़ खड़े हों।।
चाल इसकी धीमी तब होती या डूबती सागर में, जब छोड़ती निजी स्वरूप।
झूठ-चालाकी, स्वार्थ और आतंक का कूड़ा कर्कट इसमें ना कभी भरो।।

Boat of Life

The boat of life is floating in the worldly ocean
Our Creator has made it such that it is pure, light and moves smoothly
Its function is to move on, no hindrance can stop it
No matter how many difficulties come in its way
It becomes slow when it does not move according to its real nature
Keep it clean and do not fill it with untruth, selfishness, and arrogance.

2.5.12 सात्त्विक कर्म की नई परिभाषा

अधिकार, पुरस्कार की करो न चिंता।
समयानुसार सात्त्विक कर्म करो।।
पुरातन काल में वर्णधर्म को सात्त्विक कर्म कहा था।।
किन्तु अनुगीता में वर्णधर्म का उल्लेख नहीं।।
अनुगीता की नई परिभाषा 'सर्वभूतहित है सात्त्विक कर्म का लक्षण'।

New Definition of Sattvika Karma

Don't give importance to rights and awards;
Only think of the right actions, doing them at the right time
In ancient days, caste-duty was called Sattvika Karma
But Anu-Gita makes no mention of caste
Practical Vedanta accepts the new definition given in Anu-Gita
Actions that promote good-of-all, are Sattvika.

2.5.13 सच्चाई और सुगन्ध

न सच्चाई है बनावट में, न सुगन्ध है काग़ज़ के फूलों में।
सत्यता दिखाई देती है आँखों में, वातावरण शोभित होता है शब्दों से।।

आदर्श बनाते हैं वीर पुरुष, नम्रता आती विचारों से।
धन-दौलत उत्तम हैं, जब तक लगे हों जन सेवा में।।
सबसे बड़ा धर्म वही, करे दरिद्र की रक्षा मन से।
कर्म नहीं है कर्मकाण्ड में, बसा हुआ है निःस्वार्थ सेवा में।।
सच्चाई और सुगंध वहाँ है फैल रही, जहाँ सत्यता पर समाज है टिका हुआ।

Truth and Fragrance

The reality of Truth is not in hypocrisy, nor fragrance in artificial flowers
It is seen in the expression of eyes and in the atmosphere where sweet words are spoken
Wealth is precious if it is used for the service of mankind
The highest form of religion is one that teaches service of the poor
Real action is selfless and not ritualistic
Seva done by karma-yogins spreads its fragrance far and wide.

2.5.14 दुःख-सुख

दुःख, सुख सहोदर भाई हैं, छोटे-बड़े का अस्तित्व नहीं।
व्यर्थ है तुलना करना, जब दोनों हैं एक बराबर।।
कष्ट देख अन्य किसी का, जिसका हृदय पीड़ा से छिन्न हुआ।
ऐसे व्यक्ति का चेहरा प्रसन्नता से है सदा खिला हुआ।।
दुःख अधिक सताते उनको, जो सुखी देख किसी को हैं क्षीण हुए।
दुःख-सुख का यह ज्ञान गीता से सीखो।।

Pain and Pleasure

Pain and pleasure are twins, no one is younger or older
They are equal, no use comparing them
Those who feel pain, seeing the pain of anybody
Such people get happiness inside their heart
They have more suffering in life, who are unhappy seeing other people happy
Learn from Gita the art of sharing pain and pleasure.

2.5.15 मन के हारे हार है, मन के जीते जीत

कोई बसा है कारागारों में, कोई घर की चार दीवारों में।
एक भूखा सड़क किनारे बैठा है, एक पीड़ित असमर्थ है खाने में।।

परिस्थिति सबकी एक तरह की, चेहरे के भाव हैं अलग बने।
किसी के चेहरे पर मुसकान बनी, किसी की आँखों में आँसू की धार बही।।
जिसने अपने मन को जीत लिया, उसने दुःख को दूर भगा दिया।

Reconciliation

Some are in prison house, some are inside the four walls of the house
Out of hunger, some are sitting along the road, some are not able to eat
Situation is the same, expressions on face are different
Still some are smiling, while some have continuous flow of tears
Those who have reconciled, they have come out of pain

2.5.16 संन्यासी

दो प्रकार के होते संन्यासी, एक घर द्वार को छोड़ने वाले, एक गृहस्थी में रहने वाले।
पहने भगवा कपड़े, मात-पिता से नाता तोड़ा, लिया कमण्डल हाथ।।
आश्रम बना निवास है उनका, भोजन निर्भर करता औरों पर।
ज्ञान-ध्यान सिखाते सबको, त्याग-तपस्या करते हैं।।
दूसरे गृहस्थी में रहकर, संभाल समस्या जीवन की, दिन-रात व्यस्त रहते हैं।
संयम है जीवन में भारी, सहायता को सभी की हैं तत्पर।।
सहन-शक्ति कर्मों से आई, काम में लगे हुए निरन्तर।
ये संन्यासी किसी तरह कमज़ोर नहीं, इनकी भी महिमा भारी है।।

Sannyasi

There are two types of sannyasi, those who leave the family and others who live in the family
The former puts on saffron clothes and keeps no connection with parents
They live in monasteries and for food they depend on others and keep themselves busy studying scriptures
The other type are those who live in families, and keep lot of discipline in life
They work hard, learn discipline from hard work and are busy continuously

They are not less great in any way and not less admirable.

2.5.17 समाधि

न कोई चाह है, ना कोई चिन्ता है, कार्य करना है निःस्वार्थ भाव से।
फल ईश्वर आधीन है, उससे कोई लगाव नहीं।।
निन्दा-स्तुति चाहे जितनी हो, उस पर अपना अधिकार नहीं।
छोड़ दिया जिसने भाव कर्तापन का, उसको कोई भय सता न सका।।
शांत रहा सदा उसका मन, सच्ची समाधि को उपलब्ध हुआ।

Calm

Having no selfish desire and no worry, we have to work selflessly
We must not get attached to the result, it depends on the will of God
No matter how much criticism and praise we get, we must move on. It is in God's hands
Those who get rid of the feelings of burden from doing, they are not afraid of any calamity
They are always at ease and get the blissful peace.

2.5.18 आनन्द

आनन्द ढूँढ रहे हैं ताल-तलैयों पर, या कहीं पहाड़ की चोटी पर।
कोई ढूँढ रहा महलों में, कोई ढूँढ रहा है जंगल में।।
पूजा कर-कर हार गए, दान दे-दे कर थक गए।
स्वार्थ भरे किये काम में, निराशा है भरी पड़ी।।
आनन्द मिला जब अन्दर झाँका, वह तो अपने में है छिपा हुआ।
निःस्वार्थ भाव से किया काम, आशा का ना लिया नाम।।

Pleasure of Life

We are trying to find pleasure near the rivers and ponds, or on the tops of the hills and
mountains
Some are searching in palaces, some in forests
Some pray all day long, some go on giving charity
Whatever work we do with selfishness is bound to bring sadness
Pleasure comes when we think deeply, everything is inside you

Do your work selflessly, never ponder on results

2.5.19 तूफ़ानी मन

क्या यह तूफ़ान है मेरे मन का, या बाहर हुआ है झंझावात।
आँखों से मोती से आँसू टपक रहे, या बाहर हैं ओले बरस रहे।।
कितनी मन में हो रही चंचलता कितना वातावरण में है शोर हुआ।
व्याकुल मन जब हुआ बहुत, झाँका बाहर, शान्त दिखाई दिया सभी कुछ।।
मेरे मन की अशांति ने ही बनाया हुआ है वातावरण चंचल।
प्रयत्न किया, और समझाया व्याकुल मन, देखा चारों ओर शांति है छाई हुई।।

Disturbed Mind

Is this disturbance outside or is it inside me?
Are the balls of hail falling outside or are these tears falling from my eyes?
I was so anxious that I heard noise all around me
Anxiety forced me to step outside, where it was calm and peaceful
Everything looked unpleasant and torturous because of my own disturbed mind
I consoled myself, reminding myself that I can realize peace everywhere with my mind.

2.5.20 सफलता की कुंजी

रोक-टोक, पाबन्दी, आगे बढ़ने में बाधक सिद्ध हुई।
यह ज्ञान अमेरिका से मिला विश्व को, हमने भी इससे सीखा है।।
सम्मान, नम्रता और परिश्रम, भारत की है देन हमें।
दो सभ्यताओं का जहाँ हुआ है मिश्रण।।
छोड़ सभी बाधाएँ पीछे, अग्रसर होने का मार्ग मिला।

Key of Success

Too much interference and restrictions are big hindrances in the path of success
We learnt this in America, it is a big contribution of this country to the world
Kindness, respect and love we had learnt in our mother India
Harmonizing these two great cultures, we achieve success
We want to give this message

Leave all burdens behind, move on forward.

2.5.21 चार गुरु

गाँधी जी के तीन गुरु, 'बुरा न देखो', 'बुरा न बोलो', 'बुरा सुनो ना भाई'।
चौथा गुरु 'बुरा न सोचो', जैसी सोच, आँखों, कानों, और बोली ने वैसा ही साथ दिया।।
चारों में है मेल बड़ा, एक संग 'परस्पर भाव' से रहते हैं
'सर्वहित' की हो सोच, बोली पर अंकुश, आँखों में करुणा, कानों से सुन्दर शब्द सुनें।।
विश्वास जिन्हें रहता अपने पर, ईश्वर कृपा रहती उनपर।

Four Gurus

Do not see evil, do not talk evil, do not hear evil - these were the three gurus of Gandhi
We add the fourth guru - do not think evil. It controls all the senses
All these four gurus live together in great harmony
Those who think in this direction have full control on themselves and try to help everyone
Those who have confidence and faith get grace of God.

2.5.22 देश-काल-पात्र

समयानुकूल अपनी क्षमता के अनुसार जिसने है कर्म किया।
वही सफल जीवन में, जिसने पीछे मुड़कर कभी न देखा, आगे बढ़ता चला गया।।
डरा नहीं झूठी निन्दा से, प्रसन्न न हुआ चुपड़ी-चिकनी बातों से।
बनाए रखा जीवन में संयम, चाहे किसी कठिनता का करना पड़ा सामना।।
सराहनीय है ऐसे महापुरुषों का जीवन, जो ऐसी दिशा दिखाकर चले गए।
गीता का देश-काल-पात्र संदेश मानव-जाति को सिखा गए।।

Desh-Kala-Patra

Gita gave the mantra,
'Do adjust your Seva according to time, place and circumstances'
Swami Vivekananda started the process of updating Traditional Vedanta

Tagore appealed to the world —
'Give up traditional ideas of conflict and supremacy'
Gandhi gave new shape to traditional Ahimsa
To face challenges of the 21st Century
All of us must modify orthodox mentality.

2.5.23 दान

तन, मन, धन से होता दान, जिसके होते कई प्रकार।
पैसे से तोला जाता धन का दान, कहीं से आया, कहीं दिया गया।।
तन का दान सम्बन्धित है सेवा से, कर्म, परिश्रम है इसका आधार।
मन से दिया दान सात्त्विक है, कठिन है, लाभकारी है हर तरह।।
इसमें है हृदय की कोमलता, सरलता, त्याग और प्रेम।
कोई अहंकार नहीं, देने का आभास नहीं, सबको जोड़ता, एक बनाता है।।

Donation

Donation is of many types, by hard work, feelings and money
The value of money is counted by number, it comes and it is given
Hard work and service are the basis of physical effort
It is very useful in every way when it is given with feelings, although it is difficult
It depicts love, kindness and sacrifice
There is no egoism, no pressure
It unites and gives the feeling of oneness.

2.5.24 दुःख-मय मार्ग, सुखमय मंज़िल

दुःख से घबराना कैसा! इसने हमको बहुत सिखाया।
हिम्मत, साहस, सहन-शक्ति सिखाई, जीवन जीने का सबक़ सिखाया।।
जब-जब इसका आँचल पकड़ा, नई स्फूर्ति ने जन्म लिया।
परिश्रम किया, कठिनाइयाँ झेलीं, सच्चाई को समझा, आपत्ति को पार किया।।
सुख किया उसी ने अनुभव, सामना कर, संघर्ष के लिए जूझ पड़ा।
हँसते-हँसते सब झेल गया, सफलता की चोटी पर जा पहुँचा।।
दुःख से ना घबराहट हो कभी किसी को, यह तो मार्ग प्रदर्शित करता है।
सही रास्ता मिल जाता है, हम आगे बढ़ते जाते हैं।।

Courage in the Face of Difficulty

Don't be afraid of difficulties and pain! They teach a lot!
Just as when Arjuna's eldest brother Yudhishtra, son of Dharma, God of righteousness
Was entering the gates of heaven
He refused to enter without his faithful dog
Who had travelled with him through thick and thin, suffering it all
And Dharma told him:
Never be afraid of difficulties and pain, the suffering you face in life
I test the righteousness of all my children in their life's journey
Only those who can stay true to the principles of righteousness
Can bear the pain of suffering
And pass through
And so I say to you, never be shaken by life's difficulties
They teach you the way
To righteousness and eternal joy.

CHAPTER 2.6

Mutual Cooperation and Help

(परस्पर-भाव)

2.6.1 कैसी है ये होड़

तेज़ी से सब भगे जा रहे हैं, कहाँ? किधर? या फिर किसी होड़ में हैं लगे हुए?
कौन-सी है इनकी मन्जिल, कौन-सा मार्ग नज़र है आ रहा?
सन्तोष नहीं है किसी पड़ाव पर, चौराहे पर हर समय हैं खड़े हुए।
सुख शांति चाहिए या दौलत पर है ध्यान बना, किसी बात का नहीं पता।।
लगता है इस आधुनिक होड़ में, वाणी पर अंकुश चला गया।
पढ़ाई-लिखाई से इसका नहीं है नाता, केवल संयम, प्रेम ही है एक उपाय।।

Why are We So Competitive?

I see everybody running here and there continuously
I have no idea what they want to achieve
They do not find satisfaction at any place, as if they are standing at the crossroads
Sometimes I feel they have no control on their tongue and senses
And think only of competition
There seems to be no connection of this with education
Nor with worldly success
Solution may be possible in discipline and love.

2.6.2 जिसकी लाठी उसकी भैंस

दुनिया गोल है, सीमा बन्धन है, ईश्वर है कहीं दूर बसा।
उल्लंघन किया सीमा का, ईश्वर की क्या सत्ता है।।
धन-दौलत है पास हमारे, आज हमारी सत्ता है।

गोल है दुनिया, गोल हैं बातें, जिसकी लाठी, उसकी भैंस।।
अधिकार उसी के हैं सारे, जिसने उच्चारा सत्ता प्रलाप।

Today is Our Ego's Sovereignty

We think there are no boundaries, we can do whatever we want
We cross our boundaries, and think even God cannot do anything, we are at liberty
We believe we possess everything, so we have all the controls
World will go on as it is, we are capable like anything
We have all the rights, we say we are free, but it is our ego

2.6.3 'अति' शब्द बड़ा भयंकर

'अति' शब्द है बड़ा भयंकर, दु:खों का देने वाला है।
धन हो अति का या फिर हो कंगाली, दिन की गई चैन और रात हुई है काली।।
अति का ना हो लगाव, न किसी को आए कमी, दोनों निराश कर डालते हैं।
लिया किसी का अति सहारा, भरोसा अपने पर से चला गया।।
कुत्ते से किया प्रेम अधिक, सीधा मुँह को चाटेगा।
डाँटा, फटकारा सीमा से ऊपर, घायल वह कर डालेगा।।
अति से छुटकारा तब हुआ, जब मिला सन्तोष धन, सब धन लगे धूलि समान।

Idea of Too Much is Bad

The idea of too much is bad, it makes us uneasy
If we have too much money or we are too poor, we become uncomfortable
We cannot enjoy life, nor we can sleep at ease
Neither we should get attached too much with anyone nor should have too much expectations
Do not take too much advantage of others, we lose confidence
All these bring unhappiness in life
If we pamper a dog too much, it will lick your face
If you scold it too much, it will attack you
One leaves the idea of too much only when one is happy and satisfied with what one has.

2.6.4 स्वतन्त्रता की परिभाषा

84 वर्ष के दीर्घकाल में स्वतन्त्रता के नारे खूब सुने।

"स्वतन्त्रता जन्मसिद्ध अधिकार हमारा" तिलक ने स्वतन्त्रता-संग्राम में दिया नारा था।।

स्वतन्त्रता मिलने पर "स्वतन्त्र भारत" के रोज़ लगे नारे थे।

खुली हवा में, स्वतन्त्र रूप से, बच्चे-बूढ़े और जवानों ने स्वतन्त्रता के झंडे फहराए थे।।

आज स्वतन्त्रता का रूप कुछ और है बदला, सब करते स्वतन्त्रता की बात सदा।

छोटे-बड़े का मिटा भेद, उचित-अनुचित को दूर भगाया, अधिकारों की केवल बात करो।।

सब स्वतन्त्रता के बने अनुयायी, केवल अपनी स्वतन्त्रता का ध्यान रखा।

सफल वही जिसने दबाया दूसरे को, अपना स्वार्थ सिद्ध किया।।

किसको कहा जाये स्वतन्त्रता, इसका निर्णय स्वयं करो। सब स्वतंत्र हैं।।

Definition of Freedom

Slogans of freedom I have heard a lot in 84 years of my life

Freedom is our birthright, Tilak taught us during India's freedom struggle

We used to shout such slogans after India got freedom

In liberty we all—young and old—used to fly flags of liberty

Today concept of freedom has changed, it is only a shallow talk

There is no respect for old and young, only care for themselves

They think they believe in freedom, though they take care of their selfish interests

You yourself decide, what is real freedom, everybody is free.

2.6.5 सीमाएँ

इस धरती पर रहकर बाह्य-रूप से कोई स्वतन्त्र नहीं।

कोई शारीरिक वेदना से घिरा हुआ, कोई धन-अभाव में फँसा हुआ।।

किसी को बच्चों की चिन्ता, कुछ आयु से लाचार हुए।

स्वतन्त्र वही है, जिसने हर परिस्थिति में निडर बनकर समझौता है किया हुआ।।

चाहे कहीं हों, कैसे हों, मन की स्वतन्त्रता पर सदा किया भरोसा।

उसको कोई न छीन सका, यह बाहर की वस्तु नहीं।।

जब परिस्थिति को न बदल सको, क्यों न उसे स्वीकार करो?

Limitations

Outworldly, nobody can be called free
Some are short of money, some are suffering from acute pain
Some are worried about their children, some are suffering in their old age
Only those are free who have reconciled with every situation fearlessly
No matter in what situation they are, they are mentally free
If you can not change the situation, why not accept and adjust?

2.6.6 एक दूसरे पर निर्भर

परस्पर भाव पर ही टिका संसार।
एक धुरी के समान है यह, चारों ओर जिसके सब हैं घूम रहे।।
धरती, सूरज, चाँद, सितारे, घूम रहे हैं नियमित रूप से, आकर्षित होकर।
अकेले का कोई अस्तित्व नहीं, जीवन एक दूसरे पर निर्भर है।।
एक क्षण भी यदि निर्भरता छूटी, मृत्यु का संदेश आ जाता है।

Inter-Dependence

Paraspara-Bhava is controlling the wheel of life
The way the axel of the earth moves, we are also moving inter-dependently
Sun, Earth, Moon and Stars all are moving all around; all are attracted to one another
The whole creation depends on one another; nobody can stay alone
Don't try to run away from inter-dependence
Otherwise your life will end.

2.6.7 पुरुष, प्रकृति, जीवं

पुरुष, प्रकृति के मिलन से, सारा जगत है चलायमान।
समस्त कार्य प्रकृति में होते, प्रेरणा ईश्वर से मिलती है।।
कार्य-फल अर्पित परम-पुरुष को, आनन्दित हृदय मानव का होता।
जीव सब मिलकर आपस में, एक दूसरे का पालन-पोषण करते।।
पारस्परिक लेन-देन ही, प्रकृति-पुरुष का उपहार हमें।
गीता-अनुगीता की है शिक्षा।।

God, Nature and Living Beings

The whole universe is moving in order because of the unity of God and Nature
Getting inspiration from God, all activity takes place in this world
Leaving the result in Brahman's hands, human beings achieve happiness
Living beings survive by taking help from each other
Mutual cooperation is the gift of God to humanity
Both Gita and Anugita give this teaching.

2.6.8 विविधता में एकता

बड़े-बड़े राजा और महराजा आए, साधु संत हुए धरती पर।
बच्चे जवान फिर वृद्ध हुए, कोई धनी कोई कंगाल हुए।।
ईश्वर अंश सभी में एक बराबर, पशु पक्षी हों या कीट पतंगें।
सभी का अस्तित्व एक बराबर, छोटे बड़े एक समान।।
जितने सूरज, चाँद, सितारे, सभी टिके हैं उसी सहारे।
हम सब उसी का अंश लिए, हैं परस्पर - भाव से जुड़े हुए।।
याद करें बस उसी प्रभु को, जिसने हमको जन्म दिया।
एक पिता की संतान है हम, सब पर उसकी दया बराबर।।

Unity in Diversity

This world produced Lords and Kings, saints and holy men,
Children become young and then old, some become rich, some poor
God is in everyone, no matter it is animal, bird or fly,
In the eyes of God all are equal, there is no great and no one is small
Existence of sun, moon and stars, depend upon the same intelligence
We are all united because God is in all of us
Always remember Him, who gave life to all of us
He is Father of us all, so mutual cooperation is the natural way of life.

2.6.9 प्रेम-भाव

प्रेम भाव है नियति का वरदान जगत को।

पुरुष-प्रकृति के प्रेम ने ही संसार को दिया जन्म।।
बीज के दो हिस्से हैं, संग रहकर ही विकसित होते हैं।
अकेला कोई नहीं फूलता-फलता, मिट्टी में मिल जाता है।।
प्रत्येक वस्तु में है जीवन, प्रकृति से सदैव वह जुड़ी हुई।
मानव की भी हर प्राणी के साथ हो मित्रता।।
नियति ने हम सबको एक संग जोड़ा है।

Feelings of Love
Feelings of Love are a great blessing of God to the world
Our world came into existence by combining Nature with the spirit of life
A seed has two parts and they flourish mutually together
Nothing can survive alone; it will surely die and turn into dust
Life is in everything that is joined with Nature
Humans must also unite in friendship with Nature
God has created all as one.

2.6.10 परस्पर भाव की महत्ता
साइंस के इस युग में, सुख सुविधा, चमत्कार की कोई कमी नहीं।
देशों की दूरी ख़त्म हुई, ग़रमी-सर्दी का आभास नहीं।।
मनुष्य फिर भी खोया-खोया, मानसिक रोग अधिक हैं सता रहे।
अकेलापन खाता है, चिंता-भय अधिक सताते हैं।।
ध्यान करो, "परस्पर-भाव" सम्भवतः इसका एक उपाय।

Importance of Helping Each Other
There is no dearth of convenience and miracles in this scientific age
Distance between countries appears short; in homes we don't feel heat and cold
Still human beings are lost; and mental diseases are at their peak
One feels desperately lonely; worries and fears are heightened
Keep in mind the importance of helping each other;
Perhaps this might be the solution

2.6.11 एक साथ चलो
बाहर खड़ी देख रही थी, पक्षी डाल पर बैठ अकेला, काँय-काँय करता था।

करुण पुकार सुनी साथी ने, तुरन्त आया, फिर दोंनो मिल साथ चले गए।।
कुछ क्षण का अकेलापन भी कितनी पीड़ा देता है, प्राण ही हर लेता है।
दोनों कह रहे थे, साथ चलो, साथ करो, साथ हर रूप में दो।।
अकेले काँय-काँय करते रह जाएँगे, नहीं कभी कुछ कर पाएँगे।

Stay Together
Standing outside, I saw a bird sitting alone on the branch of a tree and making noise
Tone was very pathetic, partner heard and came over, then both of them went away
How much pain loneliness gives, no matter how short it is
Both of them were saying, always stay together, work together in every way
We will not be able to accomplish anything while we are alone.

2.6.12 जीवन की कुंजी

संसार टिका है एक धुरी पर, वही कर रही परिश्रम से काम निरन्तर।
समाज चल रहा है एक शब्द पर, प्रेम से होते सारे काम निरन्तर।।
'त्याग' सेवा का सूचक है, बच्चे बूढ़े सब इसी सहारे टिकते हैं।
सत्य से बढ़कर कोई धर्म नहीं, सारे धर्मों का सार यही।।
भूलो नहीं इन शब्दों को, ये सफल-जीवन की कुन्जी हैं।

Key to Life's Success
The world is moving all the time, around an axis that is continuously rotating
Society is functioning on one word. It is called Love
Old and young, depend on services from others. Indicating sacrifice from each other
There is no religion bigger than Truth. It is the essence of all the world religions
We should never forget this. It will bring us success in life.

2.6.13 सच्ची भक्ति

एक हमारा परम-पिता, एक हमारा परम-धाम।
एक जगह से आए हैं, एक जगह सबको जाना है।।
कौन है देशी, कौन है परदेशी, एक डोर में पिरोए हुए।।

आदर-सम्मान सभी को प्यारे, इससे बढ़कर कोई भेंट नहीं।
प्रेम एकता ही है भक्ति, यही है इसका सच्चा नाम।।

True Worship
Our source is one, our permanent abode is one
We have all come from Brahman and ultimately we will go to the same source
We are all one, no one is a foreigner here. We are like beads around a thread
The thread of love is so strong, it makes us all one
Everyone loves respect and regard, there is no other gift which we call more precious
Our worship is love and unity with all
That is true worship.

2.6.14 सब जुड़े हुए

अपने को समझ समान सभी के, फिर 'परस्पर' की बात करो।
मत समझो अपने को भिन्न कभी, सभी एक दूसरे पर निर्भर हैं।।
माता ने हमको जन्म दिया, पाला-पोसा बड़ा किया, पिता ने आगे हमें बढ़ाया।
सगे सम्बन्धी और पड़ौसी, सभी का लिया सहयोग निरन्तर।।
सब एक दूसरे से जुड़े हुए, अकेले का कोई अस्तित्व नहीं।

We are All Connected
Do not think yourself special. All are equal
Never think you are separate - we all depend on each other
Mother gave birth to us, raised us, worked day and night
Father helped us, taking us ahead in life
Our relatives and neighbors always supported us in our times of need
We are all connected and dependent on each other
Nobody can survive alone.

2.6.15 अपना-पराया कोई नहीं

सभी हमारे अपने हैं, या फिर कभी किसी को कहो न अपना।
अपना कहने में गम्भीर दुःख है छिपा हुआ, इससे मन में आशा बढ़ती है।।
अपना-पराया साथ हैं चलते, भेद-भाव को मन में लाते हैं।
सबको मन में समान समझ, करो सबके हित का ध्यान।।

कभी बोझ, स्वार्थ न आएगा मन पर, 'सर्व हित' की शक्ति ब्रढ़ेगी हर पल।

We are All One

Either say everyone belongs to you or say that no one is yours
If we have a feeling of possessiveness, it will bring pain and expectations
Mine and thine go together, and create the feeling of you and me in our minds
Consider everybody equal, think only about the welfare of all
You will realize there is no stress on your mind
You will always keep yourself busy in the work of social good.

2.6.16 बिन बोले निकले बोल

बिन बोले निकले बोल, बड़े क़ीमती, सच्चे हैं बोल।
हृदय के अन्तस्तल में है इनका वास, शांति दायक हैं ये बोल।।
ऊँच नीच से कोई सम्बन्ध नहीं, कटुता का तो नाम नहीं।
सीधा ईश्वर से इनका नाता, जीवन में सबको एक बनाता।।
आधार इसका है गहरा प्रेम, रूप बड़ा व्यावहारिक है, करो सबसे मेल।।

Words Without Manipulation

Words that come out without manipulation are very precious and true
They reside in inner depths of the heart, and give peace to everyone
They don't differentiate between high and low, and no question of bitterness
There is a direct connection with God, uniting everybody as one
Their foundation is deep love, and their message is practical
Be united with everyone.

2.6.17 शब्दों की महिमा

मीठे शब्द प्रेम से निकलें, घायल हृदय के घाव हैं भरते।
कड़वी बातें मुख से निकलीं, मन व्याकुल कर जाती हैं।।
मित्र तुम्हारे दूर हैं भागते, रिश्तों की डोर टूट गई।
कठिन समय में रहे खड़े अकेले, हाय-हाय के शब्द मुख से निकले।।

क्या कुछ तुम कहते हो, ध्यान बस बना रहे, सदा तुम सुखी रहोगे।

Importance of Words

Haughtiness and bitter words are worse than blades of the sword
Their wounds are so deep they break the heart into pieces
The good effect comes only when we speak at the right time and with deep thinking
When someone is silent, do not think that the other one is weak
Only those can remain quiet who have control on themselves
We should always honor the words; their importance is very great.

2.6.18 मर्यादा बनी रहे

मुख से क्या शब्द हैं निकलें, मर्यादा सदा बनी रहे।
कितना, किससे करवाया है, इसका भी ध्यान सदा रहे।।
करने की कोई नहीं है सीमा, नहीं मर्यादा मीठे शब्दों पर।
सबको कितना हम प्यार करें, इस पर भी कोई टोक नहीं।।
बुरा शब्द मुख से निकला, आजीवन पछताना पड़ता है।
शुभ चिंतक हुए सभी के, मन शांत हमारा रहता है।।

Control Yourself

Always keep in mind what words we utter
Keep in mind how much help you got from others
There is no limit on how much you do to others and how sweetly you talk
There is no limit on how deeply we love each other
You will repent lifelong if bad words come out of you
So long as we do and think well of others we are at ease

2.6.19 संयम

समाज में वही व्यक्ति ऊँचा उठता, जिसको अपनी सीमा का है ध्यान बना।
सीमा का ही नाम है संयम, इसे समाज का प्राण हैं कहते।।
प्रेम की सीमा का कोई अन्त नहीं, जितनी बढ़े उतनी ही खुशबू-कारी है।
शब्दों की सीमा का किया उल्लंघन, घातक सिद्ध हो जाती है।
अपनी सीमा में सदा रहो, यह सीख सदा चली आई है।।

Self-Discipline

Those who know their limitations can only uplift themselves in the society
Limitation brings discipline, that is why it is called essence of society
Love has no limit, more you do, more useful it becomes
Never cross the limitation of words, otherwise it will become dangerous
Mind your limitations, it is a norm of the society
This is self-discipline, not imposed by force.

2.6.20 कड़वे शब्द—तलवार की धार

अकड़ना और बोलना कड़ुवा, ये तलवार की धार से भी हैं बुरे।
इनके घाव हैं गहरे, हृदय को चूर-चूर कर देते हैं।।
शब्द समय, परिस्थिति को सोचकर बोलो, तभी प्रभावित करते हैं।
किसी और का चुप रहना, मत समझो कमज़ोरी उसकी।।
जिसने अपने मन को जीता है, वही समय पर चुप रह सकता है।
शब्दों की महिमा बड़ी, उसका सदा आदर-सम्मान करो।।

Bitter Words

Haughtiness and bitter words are worse than blades of a sword
Their wounds are so deep, they break the heart into pieces
The good effect comes only when we speak softly at the right time
When someone is silent, do not think that it is a sign of weakness
Only those can remain quiet, who have control on themselves
We should always honor words, their importance is very great

2.6.21 आदर्श जीवन

सुनी किसी की करुण पुकार, प्रेम-भाव से गले लगाया।
न हुई कभी कटुता मन में, ना किया कभी अपमान किसी का।।
सुख से विचरता रहा इसी जीवन में, चेहरा शांत बना रहा।
दिखाई दिया न कोई शत्रु कहीं, मित्रों ने सदा है घेरा डाला।।
परस्पर-भाव से प्रेरित हो, सबका सदा सहयोग मिला।
आदर्श जीवन का दुर्गम मार्ग प्रभु कृपा से सुगम हुआ।।

Glimpses of Ideal Life
To give priority to helping the poor
Not from a sense of pity, but seeing God in them
To put into practice
The Vedantic message of one-ness of all beings
To try for inter-religious harmony
This is the most urgent need of the 21st century
To try to empower women
Who have suffered for thousands of years.

2.6.22 बच्चे, बूढ़े, और जवान
बच्चे, बूढ़े और जवान, तीनों समाज का हिस्सा हैं।
तीनों का है महत्त्व बराबर, किंतु कार्यक्षमता नहीं एक समान।।
आयु से है सोच बदलती, बदलते हैं जीवन के अनुभव।
भिन्न तरह सें तीनों काम हैं करते, भिन्न प्रभाव जीवन पर पड़ते।।
तीनों पर है अन्याय, यदि आशा की जाय एक तरह की।
आयु क्षमता के साथ-साथ भावना भी बदलती रहती है।।
परिवार की सबसे बड़ी ज़िम्मेदारी-बच्चों की शिक्षा होती है।
इसका हम-सब ध्यान रखें, तभी जीवन और समाज सरलता से चलता है।।

Children, Adults, and Old People
In ancient times, we had four Ashramas
Brahmacharya, Grihastha, Vanaprastha, Sanyasa
In today's world, the last two Ashramas are not practical
Senior citizens do not leave homes
The responsibility for looking after family falls mostly on Grihastha, or adults
But old people also provide support
Giving the benefit of their long experience
Proper bringing up of children is the most important function of the family
Broad-based education of boys as well as girls is a must
No discrimination between boys and girls and no child labor
Poverty should be no bar to education and scientific education is a must.

CHAPTER 2.7

Vegan Diet for Compassionate Living

(आहार-शुद्धि और दया-भाव)

2.7.1 अनुगीता का प्रसिद्ध श्लोक

शाकाहार से भी ऊँचा स्थान, अनुगीता ने दिया अहिंसाहार को।
जिसे आजकल कहते हैं, 'वीगन'।।
अनुगीता का प्रसिद्ध श्लोक, 17.10 – भगवान की सनातन शिक्षा।
फलमूल ही है उत्तम आहार।।
वीगन के इतिहास में, होना चाहिए इस श्लोक का उल्लेख।
वीगन-शिक्षा का विश्व में प्रथम उपदेश।।

Anu-Gita's Famous Shloka

Anu-Gita Shloka 17.10 is famous, it is the oldest scriptural recommendation
Declaring a plant-based Diet as a spiritual pursuit
Anu-Gita in the Mahabharata, and selections of Shlokas from the Mahabharata
Help us understand
The roots of veganism in our world today.

2.7.2 गुण-कारी भोजन

खान-पान नहीं बाहर की वस्तु, देखा और उठाकर खा लिया।
भोजन को देख मन में कैसे विचार उठे, इस पर निर्भर करता आहार हमारा।।
शांति-प्रिय, विश्व-शांति को मानने वाला, कैसे पशु-हत्या को स्वीकार करे।
हृदय में उसके दर्द है भरता, क्या सोच वह भोजन ग्रहण करे।।
पशु प्रेम और मानसिक शांति मिलेगी इससे, जिसे खोज रहा सारा संसार।

खाओ शाकाहारी भोजन, आँखें होंगी तृप्त, अंग-अंग होगा बलवान और शांत।।

Food for the Soul
Food is not to be taken lightly
It is our sustenance, and nourishment for body and mind
In the 21st Century, the world has become
Acutely aware of the risk of destruction
The chanting of World Peace, an ever increasing mantra
Cruelty against animals now taking a turn towards violence against mankind
The vegan diet helps us live with compassion
And for the good of our world.

2.7.3 शाकाहार ही आदर्श भोजन

स्वामी विवेकानन्द के शब्दों को सुनो, उन्होंने कहा,
मैं इस समय पूर्ण शाकाहारी नहीं हूँ।
बंगाल में मेरा जन्म हुआ, किंतु वेदान्त की शिक्षा ने मुझे सचेत किया,
अब मैं पशुओं को अपना भाई समझता हूँ।
मेरा यह आदर्श है, शाकाहारी भोजन अपनाओ।।

Vivekananda' Lesson on Ideal Food
Not many people have read
Swami Vivekananda's views on ideal food.
He spoke in 1896,
The ideal is not to eat flesh, not to injure any being
For all animals are my brothers, and all life is sacred
If you can think of other forms of life as your brothers,
You have made a little headway
Towards the brotherhood of all souls
And the teaching of Vedanta.

2.7.4 आइन्स्टाइन का समर्थन

स्वामी विवेकानन्द ने 1896 में कहा था,
व्यावहारिक वेदान्त में, धर्म और विज्ञान मिलेंगे।
यह भविष्यवाणी साक्षात्कार हुई, आइन्स्टाइन के समर्थन से।।
"ज्यों-ज्यों मानवजाति शाकाहार को अपनाएगी,
त्यों-त्यों संसार में मानवजीवन का अस्तित्व सुदृढ़ होगा।

और सबके स्वास्थ्य में सुधार भी आएगा।।"

Einstein's Support

Vivekananda defined Practical Vedanta
As a handshake between religion and science.
This idea gained support from Einstein:
"Nothing will benefit human health
and increase the chances for survival of life on Earth
As much as the evolution to a vegetarian diet."

2.7.5 शाकाहारी है मानव

मानव बना पाँच तत्व का पुतला, क्षिति, जल, पावक, गगन, समीरा।
दन्त बने हैं शाकाहारी भोजन को, आँखें बनी हैं करुण रस बरसाने को।।
शरीर के अन्य अंग भी कह रहे हैं, कहानी हमारी भिन्न है, नहीं माँसाहारी पशुओं जैसी।
दया, दान और तप के लिये बना है मानव, सीधी-सच्ची सोच ही है जीवन।।
दया करें सब जीव-जन्तु पर, आगे बढ़ना है लक्ष्य हमारा।
हम शाकाहारी मानव हैं, हितकारी हैं, संग सभी का देने वाले हैं।।

Through Evolution, Human is Vegetarian

Evolution gave the natural structure to humankind
Teeth are made to chew plant-based food
Eyes are made to weep with kindness and compassion
Our digestive system is not suitable for animal-based food
The human heart is naturally compassionate
Our nature is to love animals
Killing animals is against human nature.

2.7.6 स्वास्थ्य हितकारी भोजन का रहस्य

परम्परागत भोजन का भोग लगाया, शरीर फिर भी अस्वस्थ बना रहा।
कौन-कौन सी ग़लती किसने खाई, कौन-कौन कर्त्तव्य नहीं निभाया।।
नमक मसालों और मीठे पर दिया ज़ोर, ब्लड-प्रेशर कॉलेस्ट्रोल को ना देखा।
किस भावना से सजाई गई है थाली, क्या पशु-प्रेम पर आधारित थी।।
कैसी आकृति भोजन समय बनी है चेहरे की, कितनी करुणा छलक रही है आँखों में।
संतुलित और शाकाहारी भोजन ही, शारीरिक एवं मानसिक बल देता है।।

Does Your Diet Reflect Compassion?
Traditionally, taste was the test of 'good' food
Emphasis was on spices, butter, sugar, and salt
No attention on blood pressure or cholesterol
No strict avoidance of non-vegetarian food
Remember, if any animal is killed to feed you
Its misery and bleeding heart is on your conscience
Too much fat, salt, or sugar are bound to hurt you
Healthy vegan food is recommended by all for a better tomorrow.

2.7.7 अनुशासन-पर्व में माँस-भक्षण का विरोध
महाभारत में अनुशासन-पर्व को शान्तिपर्व - भाग-दो के रूप में
उच्च स्थान दिया है वेद-व्यास ने।
अनुशासन-पर्व के तीन अध्याय 13.114, 13.115, 13.116
प्रभावशाली ढंग से करते हैं विरोध माँस-भक्षण का, पशु हत्या का।
हमने इनका वर्णन किया है संस्कृत-अंग्रेज़ी दोनों भाषाओं में
विश्व-शान्ति के लिए, जगत में हो इस ग्रन्थ का प्रचार।

Teaching from Anushasana-Parva Against Animal-Based Diet
Anushasana-Parva is like Part II of Shanti-Parva in the Mahabharata
Three chapters of Anushasana-Parva, 13.114, 13.115 and 13.116
Strongly condemn eating of animal meat
To read these chapters in Sanskrit and English
We have included them in our "Selections from the Mahabharata"

2.7.8 शान्तिपर्व में पशुबलि का विरोध
शान्तिपर्व में नौ गीताएँ - लोकमान्य तिलक ने किया उल्लेख।
हमने इनका विवरण लिखा, संस्कृत-अंग्रेज़ी दोनों भाषाओं में।।
पशुबली का विरोध करने वाली विचख्नु गीता का करो प्रचार।
महाभारत के श्लोक 12.265.1 से 12.265.11 तक के ग्यारह श्लोक
देते हैं प्रभावशाली उपदेश—रोको पशुबली को विश्वशान्ति के लिए।।

Shanti-Parva Denounces Animal Sacrifice
Lokmanya Tilak wrote, there are nine Gita's (songs) in Shanti-Parva
We have presented them in Sanskrit and English
In our work "Selections from the Mahabharata"
Vichakhnu - Gita is one of the nine Gita's
It has eleven Shlokas - 12.265.1 - 12.265.11
These Shlokas make a strong appeal
"For peace on earth - stop all animal sacrifice".

2.7.9 अहिंसा-रूपी चौपाई

अनुशासन-पर्व के श्लोक 13.114.8 में
अहिंसा की व्याख्या की है चौपाई के रूप में।
मन-वचन-कर्म की महत्ता तो सभी ग्रन्थों ने सिखाई है।।
किन्तु अनुशासन-पर्व के अनुसार यह व्याख्या पूर्ण नहीं है।
अहिंसा तिपाई नहीं, चौपाई है, और चौथा पाया है - शाकाहार।।

Veganism is Part of Ahimsa
Anushasan-Parva Shloka 13.114.8 has defined Ahimsa
As a four-legged stool.
Thought, word, and deed are the three legs known to all
But veganism is the fourth leg of Ahimsa

2.7.10 जड़ी-बूटी की चाय

फूल-पत्ते, शहद-मसाले, जड़-टहनी का है चूरा इसमें।
स्वाद की दृष्टि से कभी मिलाया गुड़ या फिर नींबू का रस इसमें।।
पीकर चेतनता लगी है बढ़ने, स्फूर्ति आई अंग-अंग में।
काम करने की बढ़ी है शक्ति, आलस्य का है नाम नहीं।।
रंग प्राकृत, नहीं कोई मिलावट नक़ली इसमें।
जितना चाहो करो इसका सेवन, नींद संतुलित आती है।।
जानवरों का दूध नहीं मिलाया जाता इसमें।
अपना ही स्वाद हितकारी और अनोखा है।।
यह बड़ी सरल, लाभकारी और सुख देने वाली पूँजी है।।

Herbal Tea
Made with herbs, roots, honey and spices

Herbal tea gives you a new sense of vigor in your daily routine
Free of chemicals, or animal milk
It is invigorating and healthy, full of nutrients and pleasing to taste
Cha-No-You of Japan made tea famous
With the Chinese word *chaa* modified in the West
Herbal tea is free from caffeine
And millions are now fond of vegan herbal tea

2.7.11 घी के विषय में पूछो डॉक्टरों से

भारतीयों का स्वास्थ्य चिन्ता का विषय है।
और इसका एक कारण है—जो भोजन हमने सदा से खाया है।।
यदि हम चाहते हैं कि हमारी नई पीढ़ियों का स्वास्थ्य अच्छा हो।
तो हमें डाक्टरों से पूछना चाहिए, विशेषत: घी के विषय में।।

Doctor's Advice on Use of Ghee
Doctors Enas and Kannan's book
"How to beat the heart disease epidemic"
Is a must read for South Asians
They have advised improvement in the way of cooking
To avoid ghee and frying techniques
For a healthy and vegan way of healthy living
Especially based on their study of South Asians

2.7.12 हे पशुपतिनाथ के भक्तों

पशुपतिनाथ का भव्य मंदिर, हमें भी दर्शन का सौभाग्य प्रभुकृपा से मिला।
वहाँ बन्दरों ने हमारे हाथ से पूजा की मिठाई को स्वयं स्वीकार कर लिया।।
क्योंकि पशु के रूप में वे भगवान ही थे। ज़रा सोचो!
पशु-हत्या पूजा नहीं हो सकती।।
महाभारत में लिखा है—पशु हत्या से पूजा करने वाले।
स्वयं माँस खाने के लिए पूजा का ढोंग भी करते हैं।।

O, Devotees of Pashupatinath
By God's grace, we visited Pashupatinath temple
Monkeys were enjoying, jumping and playing
Stealing our offerings for their mid-day snack

Monkeys are also devotees of the Lord
How can true devotees sacrifice animals in the name of the Lord?
So says the Mahabharata.

2.7.13 हे पालतू जानवरों को प्यार करने वाले

हे पालतू जानवरों को प्यार करने वाले!
ज़रा सोचो, प्यार का अर्थ क्या है?
प्यार और करुणा को अलग नहीं कर सकते।
अर्थात् प्यार और अहिंसा अभिन्न हैं।।
पशुओं को प्यार करने वाले।
पशु हत्या नहीं कर सकते।।
नहीं तो तुम आडम्बरी कहलाओगे!

O, Lovers of Pets!

O, lovers of pets! What is the meaning of your love for animals?
Compassion is an essential element of love
Love and non-violence are two sides of the same coin
How can pet-lovers bear to kill and eat animals?
It is against the nature of love.

CHAPTER 2.8

Gita, Anu-Gita, Shanti-Parva

(गीता, अनुगीता, शांतिपर्व)

2.8.1 गीता-अनुगीता

गीता निचोड़ है धर्म ग्रन्थों का, अनुगीता उसका सरल रूप।
दोनों ने मिल एक साथ दिशा दिखाई, दिया निराला रूप।।
ज्ञान दिया, निडर बनाया, जीने का ज्ञान सिखाया।
कर्म को प्राथमिकता दी, अन्ध विश्वास ढोंग से हमें बचाया।।
दया, प्रेम, भाई-चारे से आगे बढ़ना सिखलाया।
यह है "गीता-अनुगीता" की देन हमें, पढ़ो दिन-रात इन्हें।।

Gita-Anugita

Gita is the essence of our scriptures, and Anu-Gita is its simplified form
Together they show us the right path to follow in life
They give us deep knowledge, make us fearless and teach us the art of living
They give importance to Seva, and to Paraspara-bhava
That is, mutual cooperation and help
We must follow them whole-heartedly at all times.

2.8.2 सब एक हैं

हम सब एक हैं, नहीं दूसरा कोई।
ना कोई है अपना, ना कोई पराया।।
यह भाव उदित होते ही मन में।
सेवा-भाव उठा हृदय में।।
सब प्राणी से हुआ प्यार।

हीन का कहीं प्रश्न नहीं।।
जब यह विचार बना रहे निरन्तर।
समझो! गीता को है समझ लिया।।

All are One

We are all one, we are not different
We all belong to each other, we are not separate
As soon as this idea comes to our mind
We get the urge for serving everyone
We have love for the poor in particular
If you always have this feeling in your mind and heart
You have realized the truth, you have understood the Gita.

2.8.3 हम कौन हैं?

जन्म-भूमि को छोड़, कर्म भूमि में रहते हैं।
सगे सम्बन्धी दूर हैं बैठे, ध्यान उनका रखते हैं।।
कठिन परिश्रम, प्रेम भाव से, मन लगाकर रहते हैं।
आगे बढ़ने की इच्छा मन में, सबको समान समझते हैं।।
इसी ध्येय को रखकर मन में सत्-कर्म में हैं लगे हुए।
कर्म सन्देश 'गीता' से पाया, सरल किया अनुगीता ने।।

Who are We?

We left our birthplace and are living in workplace
Our relatives, live very far away, but we think about them
With the feeling of love, work very hard with a feeling of satisfaction
We think everybody alike and try to go forward
Keeping such things in mind, keep ourselves busy doing good deeds
We learnt theory of actions through Gita, of course Anu Gita made it easy.

2.8.4 काम का आनन्द

काम करने का आनन्द तभी, जब कर्तापन का हो ध्यान नहीं।
अहंभाव जमाकर किए काम से क्या कोई प्रसन्न हुआ कभी।।
स्वार्थ से किया काम गीता-विरुद्ध है, समाज विरुद्ध है।

स्वयं का हित इसमें नहीं छिपा, औरों को कष्ट बहुत मिला।।
धर्म विरुद्ध है यह स्वार्थ भाव, भविष्य में दुःख देने वाला है।

Enjoyment in Work
Work is enjoyable when we are free from arrogance
When the doer does work with self-importance, the pleasure of that work is lost from the one who does and the one who receives
Doing the work with selfish motive is against society and Gita
Neither does it do good to others, nor it helps us, and it is against dharma
Selfish thought gives pain in present and future both.

2.8.5 शांति

बड़े समय तक तुझको खोजा, शांति तू नहीं मुझे दी खड़ी दिखाई।
मन के अन्दर जब गहरी डुबकी मारी, एक कोने में तू बैठी थी।।
कहा तूने मुझसे, क्यों समय व्यर्थ करती है पगली।
छोड़ बाहर के आडंबर सारे, सुथरा कर मन अपना, स्वाभाविक काम में लगी रह सदा।।
हर जगह, हर घड़ी मैं सदा तेरे साथ रहूँगी, एक बार करके तो देख!

Peace
Oh Peace, I was searching you for long. I couldn't find you anywhere
I searched you in the depth of my heart and found you sitting in a corner
You asked, why I am searching and wasting my time
Do not try to find me in the outer world; keep your heart pure
Always keep yourself busy in your natural way of life and work
All the time and every minute I will be with you; try and experiment.

2.8.6 बच्चे गगन के पक्षी

बच्चे गगन के पक्षी, ऊँची उड़ान भरते।
पंख उनके हैं निकले, पकड़ने की करो न कोशिश।।
तुम्हारा हक़ था पूरा, जब तक कला थी सीखी।

अब तुमसे मुक्त हुए परिवार भी है दूजा।।
ईश्वर का नियम है, हर स्थिति क्षणिक है।
हर कुछ यहाँ धरोहर, परिस्थिति बदलती जाती।।
सभी को कहो अपना, या नहीं कोई अपना।
सुख शांति इसी में, यही है अधिकार अपना।।

Children Birds of the Sky

Children are like flying birds; they fly at great heights
Their wings have spread; don't try to capture them
You had all the rights till you were grooming them
Now they belong to someone else and they have their own family
According to God's law, every situation changes with time
Everything is temporary; situations change rapidly
You can only say either everybody is mine or nobody is mine
Nothing in between
The only way to get peace is to recognize that all is transitional.

2.8.7 माया तेरी विचित्र कहानी

मैं माया हूँ, ठगनी मेरा नाम, मेरी बड़ी विचित्र कहानी है।
जिसके पास गई, वह भी ठगा सा रह गया, जहाँ से चली गई वह धरती पर पटक गया।।
जिसने मुझे धरोहर समझा, उसके सदा आई काम।
निरन्तर संभालकर रखा, सही जगह, सही काम में मुझे लगाया।।
सारे उसके काम हैं निकले, फिर किसी और को जा संभलाया।
ऐसी जगह मैं लक्ष्मी हूँ, बढ़ाने में सहायक और प्रसन्नता की देने वाली हूँ।

Story of Wealth

I am wealth, I put everybody in illusion, I am unique and extraordinary
One who has me, is lost; those who don't have are also miserable
Those who think I am with them for a short while, there I am useful
Such people keep me properly, at the right place and use me for the right cause

They fulfill all their desire and work; in the end they give me to someone else
I am very useful with such people; I give them happiness and take them forward

2.8.8 याद करो महापुरुषों को
राज-महल को छोड़ बुद्ध ने, ज्ञान का पाठ पढ़ाया था।
भंगी-बस्ती में रहकर गाँधी ने, दोनदुखी से नाता जोड़ा था।।
देश के कारण लाजपत, भगत सिंह ने, जान की बाज़ी खेली थी।
कृष्ण प्रेम में मीरा ने ज़हर का प्याला पीया था।।
इन सबने महान्-उद्देश्य को लेकर, देश का मान बढ़ाया था।
आज समय आ गया है, त्याग-पूर्ण काम निभाने का।।
हमारे पास महान् ग्रन्थ हैं - गीता, अनुगीता जैसे, करो इनका पाठ सदा।

Remember Great Souls
Buddha left his palace to give deep knowledge to the world
Gandhi lived with slum scavengers to establish relationship with them
For the sake of the country, Lajpat and Bhagat Singh sacrificed their lives
Having love for Lord Krishna, Meera drank poison
All these great souls gave honor to the country, keeping high ideals
Now the time has come again to sacrifice and do hard work
We have great books to learn from, like Gita and Anu Gita.

2.8.9 समानता
झड़ रहे पतझड़ में पत्ते, कुछ पीले, कुछ हरे-भरे डाली से।
सूखे पत्ते उड़े जा रहे हैं, धरती उपजाऊ करने को।।
पीले पत्ते कर रहे हैं मज़बूत तने जड़ पेड़ों के ।
हरे पत्ते किसी से कम नहीं, पशु-पक्षी का भरते पेट।।
कोई बड़ा न कोई छोटा, सब कर रहे नियम से अपना काम।
यही सिखाती अनुगीता, जो है पढ़ने योग्य सर्वैः।।

All are Equal
In fall leaves are falling from branches, some are dry, some are yellow and some are green

Dry leaves are withering to make the land fertile
Yellow leaves are strengthening roots of the trees·
Green leaves are equally important, animals satisfy their hunger
No one is great or small; everyone is doing their work in a rightful manner
Read AnuGita, it advises us to understand this.

2.8.10 देने की महत्ता

चित्त का शुद्धीकरण, मन की प्रसन्नता मिलती है देने में।
नहीं कभी भी सुख मिलता है लेने में, हाथ बढ़ाने में।।
भरोसा जो रखे स्वयं पर, दिन दूना रात चौगुना पाता है।
जनक को याद कराती पत्नी, अनुगीता में उच्च स्वर में।।

Importance of Giving

Our heart and mind get peace when we give
Comfort is not in making demands
Those who have confidence in themselves, get more and more
They themselves get great peace, others also get happiness
Janak's wife reminds her husband the importance of it in AnuGita in forceful words

2.8.11 सब एक हैं

पुरुष प्रकृति का हुआ मिलन, प्राणी ने है जन्म लिया।
दोनों मिल जब एक भए, एक सूत्र में पिरोए गए।
हर प्राणी माला का दाना, ईश्वर अंश का है धागा।।
परस्पर भाव और एकता ने हम सबको लाकर जोड़ दिया।
'अनुगीता' ने इस भाव को बार-बार दोहराया है।

All are One

Life appears, when spirit and nature meet
When they become one, like beads around a thread
God is present in every life, so everyone is like a bead of a string
Having unity and giving helping hand to each other unites everyone deeply
Anu-Gita describes it again and again.

2.8.12 अनुगीता का महत्त्व

कृष्ण ने महाभारत के महायुद्ध बीच, अर्जुन को गीता का उपदेश दिया।
शान्ति स्थापित होने पर, अर्जुन के आग्रह पर अनुगीता का पाठ पढ़ाया।।
दोहराई गई गीता की आवश्यक बातें, और कहे गए बहुत से नए विचार।
बल दिया गया जीने की विधि पर, जिसमें निहित परस्पर भाव और जातिभाव का त्याग।।
अनुगीता का महत्त्व इसी से, जो है पढ़ने योग्य सर्वैः।

Importance of AnuGita

Lord Krishna gave teachings of Gita to Arjun on the battle field
After peace was established, Arjun insisted on learning Gita again
By that time Krishna did not repeat many things, but told some new and some old teachings
He emphasized, how one should lead a good life, which means helping one another, and no concept of caste
This very idea made AnuGita so important.

2.8.13 गीता का पूरा सन्देश

प्राचीन काल के विद्वानों ने कहा—गीता मोक्षशास्त्र है।
यह था अधूरा ज्ञान। स्वामी विवेकानन्द ने कहा।
गीता से जगत्-हित का संदेश सीखा।
महात्मा गांधी ने गीता का पूरा संदेश समझा -
और देश को गुलामी से मुक्त किया।

The Complete Message of the Gita

Ancient scholars interpreted Gita as moksha-Shastra
This was obviously not the complete message
Swami Vivekananda removed this error —
He said, "The complete message is good-of-all"
Mahatma Gandhi's commentary explained this to all Indians in Gujarati
By following Gandhi, India's colonization was ended.

2.8.14 प्रेम भिन्न है आसक्ति से

जो भी अपने सम्पर्क में आए, प्यार सभी के संग गहरा हो अपना।

आसक्ति जितनी कम, उतनी अच्छी, यह सीख गीता से पाई।।
प्यार सत्य है जितना, आसक्ति असत्य है उतनी।
आसक्ति के पंजे गहरे, बड़ा कठिन है उससे बचना।।
इसके विपरीत प्रेम सहज है, सरल है। इसे अपनाना सही मार्ग है अपना।
सुख, शांति का देने वाला, सबको निकट बनाने वाला है।।

Love, not Attachment

It is useful to understand
The difference between love and attachment
As taught in the Gita
Attachment carries with it keen desire for the fruit of action
Which often leads to use of unfair means to achieving ends
As against this
Love is spontaneous, unconditional
That is, therefore, with no expectation of reward
It is pure. Brings peace. And it unites.

2.8.15 शांतिपर्व विश्व-शांति का संदेश

सुनो और सबको सुनाओ -
महाभारत के शांतिपर्व में, श्लोक 12.94.1 में
विश्वशान्ति का संदेश।
अन्तर्राष्ट्रीय झगड़ों का संतोषप्रद समाधान -
अहिंसा से हो सकता है, युद्ध के द्वारा नहीं।
इस प्राचीन संदेश को—बीसवीं शताब्दी में -
कार्यान्वित करने का श्रेय -
महात्मा गांधी को।।

Message of World Peace in Shanti-Parva

Look carefully —
In Shloka 12.94.1 in Shanti-Parva of Mahabharata
It gives a clear message of World peace
Wars cannot provide a satisfactory solution of international disputes
You need Ahimsa for that
The applicability of this ancient message
Was demonstrated in the 20th century

Mahatma Gandhi was the manifestation of that.

2.8.16 आत्मोद्धार

अत्याचार, कटुवाणी, दुर्व्यवहार, तामसिक भोजन, प्रिय होता तामसिक वृत्ति वाले को।
सबका अनर्थ होता है उससे, अपने को विनाश की ओर ले जाता है।।
राजसी अवस्था, है बीच की, कभी किसी का अच्छा होता, और कभी कष्ट का कारण होता।
अधिकतर प्राणी इस श्रेणी में होते, सामान्य विचार इनके हैं होते।।
सात्त्विक वृत्ति के व्यक्ति हैं बहुत कम, पर समाज उन्हीं पर टिकता है।
सदा करते सत् कर्म, सबके सहायक, सात्त्विक वृत्ति के अधिकारी हैं।।
थोड़ी मात्रा में, तीनों गुण हर व्यक्ति में होते, इनसे ऊपर उठना है।
हों ऐसे कर्म सभी के, तामसिक से राजसी और फिर सात्त्विक की ओर क़दम उठें।।

Gita Chapter 6 - Arise, Awake, Become Gunatita

Gita Chapter 6 is inspirational, it says,
You yourself are your enemy!
And you yourself are your friend
All three Gunas (qualities) form part of your nature
Make whole-hearted effort to ride up the ladder of Gunas
Practice Karma - Bhakti - Jnana - Dhyana
By persistent effort, you can rise from Tamasika to Rajasi
And then to Sattvika
Even the highest state - Gunatita - can be attained by all.

2.8.17 दैवासुर संग्राम-वृत्र-गीता

व्यक्तिगत जीवन तेज़ी से बढ़ता जा रहा है, स्वार्थ इससे है जुड़ा हुआ।
हर कोई है भयभीत हुआ, कहीं कोई है हमको लूट रहा।।
परिश्रम किया है हमने, क्यों कोई लाभ का हिंस्सा ले।
ईर्ष्या फैलने लगी समाज में, होड़ की ओर मानव दौड़ पड़ा।।
प्रेम घटता दिखाई दे रहा सभी को, निंदा का बोल-बाला है बढ़ा हुआ।
किस जगह इसका होगा अंत?
इसका उत्तर दिया श्री अरविन्द ने वृत्र-गीता के आधार पर।
उन्होंने कहा, भगवान् के भक्त कभी निराश नहीं होते।।

दैवासुर संग्राम में स्वयम् वृत्रासुर ने कहा था -
जब मैंने भगवान् को देवताओं को हिम्मत प्रदान करते देखा।
तब मुझे विश्वास हो गया कि अन्त में असुर ही पराजित होंगे।।

Lessons from Vritrasur's Gita in the Mahabharata

Shanti-Parva contains Vritra-Gita
The occasion was the ancient war
Between devas and asuras, i.e. between gods and demons
The demon leader Vritra saw ups and downs
Then surprisingly, he uttered Gita-like words
Veda Vyasa called it Vritra-Gita
Vritrasur said, I saw Narayana telling the devas
"Don't lose heart, I am with you!"
I remember this when I see how hostile person to person has become
Even as we get old we see selfishness, greed, alienation between brothers
You work hard all your life, only to fear being cheated in your old age
By those that have played no part in your efforts
Love is being lost everywhere, being replaced with insults and taunts
Where will this end?
Perhaps the answer lies in Vritrasur's Gita
Goodness will reign over evil in the end.

2.8.18 अहंकार, ईर्ष्या, क्रोध पर विजय

ईर्ष्या जड़ है अहंकार की, क्रोध की, इससे उपज रही है वैर-भावना।
पढ़ाई-लिखाई बढ़ रही तेज़ी से, वैर भावना में कमी नहीं दे रही दिखाई।।
पैसा बढ़ता जा रहा है, लेकिन एकाकीपन ने समाज को है घेर लिया।
हर कोई अपने को सिद्ध करने में लगा हुआ, औरों का ध्यान है मिटा हुआ।।
सम्बन्ध कमज़ोर होते जा रहे हैं, निवारण कैसे हो इस अहंकार रोग का।
ईर्ष्या का बोल-बाला कम होगा, जब स्वार्थ से हटकर जन सेवा की ओर ध्यान बढ़ेगा।।
क्रोध भी तभी कम होता है, जब अपनी महत्ता मन में कम हो, सबको समान समझने की इच्छा हो।

ये तीनों रोग हैं ऐसे, जो पतन की ओर प्रवाहित करते हैं।। बचकर रहो!
ऐसे हों प्रयत्न हमारे, छूट जाये नकारात्मक बातें।। आगे बढ़ते चलो!

Victory Over Arrogance, Jealousy and Anger - Lessons from Kalidas

I was impressed by Kalidas' dialogue with a Samnyasin—a monk
The monk, who lived in a cave boasted
"I have conquered anger!"
Kalidas said: "Conquering anger in a cave!
That's meaningless. Come and live in the city and show me how
I will honor you if you conquer anger where people can annoy you in a city!"
This is what I remember every day when I see anger, jealousy and arrogance all around
Education, wealth, accomplishments, they are all meaningless
How can I learn not to be driven by selfishness, greed and anger
The only path is in the service of others
With humility and compassion. Move forward with these!

2.8.19 मन पर विजय

स्वतन्त्र कौन है?
जो इन्द्रियों पर विजय पा न सका, वह स्वतन्त्र नहीं, परतन्त्र हुआ।
चाहे रहो कारागारों में, या रहो राज-महलों में, इसका ना मन पर प्रभाव हुआ।।
जो भी मन का राजा है, उसकी स्वतन्त्रता ना कोई छीन सका।
सदा जनक रहे राजा बनकर, मन से सदा अनासक्त।।
वह ज्ञानी थे, त्यागी थे, अपने मन के राजा थे, जनता के सेवक थे।
सदा उनका नाम रहा अमर, वे बलिदानी थे, मन के अंकुश धारी थे।।
स्वतन्त्र वही जिसने मन को जीता है, इन्द्रियों के वश में न हुआ कभी।

Swaraj is Victory Over Self

Who is free?
Gandhi Ji defined Swaraj as a Practical Vedantin
Swaraj literally means "Victory over Self"

People understood Gandhian Swaraj only as political independence
But the vision remains unfulfilled
As Swaraj is the ultimate emancipation attained by Janak
Exemplified by his acts of sacrifice, life of equanimity, service to all
One who can not control the distraction from senses, can never be truly free.

2.8.20 निमित्त-मात्रं भव

मेरी नैया उस पार उतारो, उतराई पूरी दे दूँगी।
स्वयं तो चुपचाप हो बैठे, पतवार मुझे सौंपी है।।
चला रहे हो, जानती हूँ, फिर मैं थकी क्यों हो जाती हूँ?
शायद अपना अस्तित्व मैं भूल रही, कर तो कोई और रहा।
जिस दिन मेरा अहंकार मिटेगा, चाल इसकी दूनी होगी।।
कोई काम न छोड़ूंगी, जो-जो तुमने सौंपा है।
वह मेरी उतराई होगी, प्रसन्नता से नदियाँ पार करूँगी।।

God is the Doer

Sitting in my life boat, why am I feeling tired?
The river bank is not yet near
Why should I feel arrogant or full of ego at my achievements?
When I know that God is the ultimate doer
Practical Vedanta places special emphasis on Gita-Shloka 11.33
Which says, to consider oneself as the doer shows egoism and arrogance
Consider yourself only as an instrument - *"Nimittta"* in Sanskrit
Because in reality, God is the doer.

CHAPTER 2.9

Grace of God

(प्रभु का सहारा)

2.9.1 ईश्वर भरोसा

जब हुआ भरोसा ईश्वर पर, सारे दुख हैं दूर भगे।
मन हुआ निश्चिन्त, हिम्मत आई अपने में।।
अंश दिखाई दिया प्रभु का सब में, सहायक बने एक दूसरे के।
वातावरण छा गया प्यार का, अपने संग सभी खड़े हुए।।
अपना-पराया ना दिया दिखाई, एक सूत्र में हैं सब पिरोए हुए।
सब कुछ कर रहा निराकार है, सही सत्य को जान लिया।।

Surrender to God

As I surrender to God, all my pain vanishes
I become peaceful, and get strength
I realize everybody is a child of God, and we all depend on each other
Love is everywhere, truth is all around
We are all united.
No one is alone, we are all in His hands.

2.9.2 अन्तस्तल की पुकार

जब-जब अंत:तल से आवाज़ है आई, शुभ हुए हैं सारे काम।
प्रभु ने अवतरित होकर जगत्‌हित किया और कराए समस्त काम।।
किया भरोसा केवल उस प्रभु पर, जिसने सुन्दर दिये विचार।
फल का न हुआ ध्यान कभी, ना स्वार्थ कभी मन में आया।।
सफलता ईश्वर अधीन है छोड़ी, स्वयं को सर्व-हित कार्य में व्यस्त किया।
मन को मिली शान्ति, सारा वातावरण शान्त हुआ।।

Inner Voice
I got success whenever I heard my inner voice
All great people and incarnations of God did work for the good of all
Not only did they do such work alone but also with others
I depend on God, who gives good thoughts
Never do I have any selfishness in mind, nor do I have any desire for personal gain
Always busy for the service of others, success and failure is in the hands of God
I get peace myself, I have nothing but social service in my mind.

2.9.3 संकट मोचन भगवान

चार साल में जो सीख गई, ना सीख सकी 80 वर्षों में।
दुख ने जब चारों ओर है घेरा डाला, केंद्रित हुआ मन उलझन सुलझाने में।।
जिधर आँख उठाकर देखा, अंधकार दिखाई देता था।
सांसारिक साधन पर किया भरोसा, निराशा और प्रतारणा का किया सामना।।
चारों ओर द्वार थे बंद हुए, एक किरण सूरज की दी दिखाई।
डरो नहीं, ना हो दुखी, कर भरोसा मेरे ऊपर, हिम्मत से तू कर काम।।
काम में है अधिकार तेरा, निर्णय सब मेरा है।
तत्काल लगा मुझको ऐसा, सब काम सही लगे हैं होने।।
मिटने लगे संशय सारे, चारों ओर सब अपने खड़े दिए दिखाई।

God is the Savior
What I could not learn in 80 years, I learnt in four
I was surrounded by pain and suffering, did not know how to escape
Everywhere I saw darkness, tried to solve problems by all means I could find
I could not find a way out, till I saw a ray of hope
Heard from the Almighty, "Do not fear. Do not lose heart. Have faith in me.
You have the right only to keep making an effort in your life, but the end is in my hands."
Immediately I realized the way out of my struggles and I found peace

My doubts disappeared and I could see help coming from all sides.

2.9.4 मैं रक्षक काहू को डरना

मँझधार में थे फँसे हुए, काली घटा थी छाई हुई, चाँदनी का कहीं नाम न था।
रास्ता नज़र न आता था, भारी थी घबराहट, मन संशय से था भरा हुआ।।
अचानक दूर क्षितिज से आवाज़ आई – कह रही थी।
"मैं रक्षक काहू को डरना" – देखो! हम किनारे पर हैं खड़े हुए।।

I am Your Protector, Do not Be Afraid

We were in great difficulty, darkness everywhere
No ray of hope seemed to be anywhere
We were fumbling with fear of uncertainty, situation was hopeless
All of a sudden I heard, as if somebody was calling from unknown
"I am watching you, have faith, do not get afraid,"
Soon we found ourselves safe in the hands of our Protector.

2.9.5 भगवान बोल रहा है

सुबह को जब आँख खुली, तू खड़ा हुआ था पास मेरे।
बोला! "मत ले हाथ में माला तू, ना कर मन्दिर जाने की बात।।
मैं भावों का राजा हूँ, उठ! कर अपने निज के काम सदा।
जैसी जिसकी रही भावना, उसमें चार चाँद लगाता हूँ।।
युक्ति, भक्ति, शक्ति का दाता हूँ, अपनी रुचि, योग्यता को लेकर कर तू काम।
इसको समझूँगा पूजा मेरी, इसको समझूँगा भक्ति मेरी"।।

Listen to God's Words

I got up in the morning and saw you standing next to me
You said, "Do not hold a garland of beads, do not think about going to temple,
I am the Lord of feelings, keep yourself busy with your daily duties
I will take you forward, whatever you do with sincere feelings
According to your talent and instinct, I give strength, faith and capability
I will always think that is your prayer and this is your faith in me."

2.9.6 प्रभु मेरा हाथ थामना

रात हो काली, घनघोर हों बादल, विपदा ने जब घेरा डाला हो।
रास्ता नज़र न आता हो, दुःख का चारों ओर बसेरा हो।।
हाथ में दिए की ले रोशनी, तुम मेरा मार्ग प्रदर्शित करना।
मुझे नहीं विश्वास किसी पर, तू ही मेरा हाथ थामना।।
सदा तूने मार्ग दिखाया, आगे भी है तेरा सहारा।
मेरी हर कमज़ोरी दूर भगे, तुझमें मेरा अटल विश्वास रहे।।

Depend on God
Whenever we are surrounded by pain and suffering
And know not what direction we follow. I request,
Show me the right path by holding a lamp in your hand
Except you, I don't have confidence in anyone else
Always you have showed me my way. I depend on you.
I pray to you, keep me firm in my faith and always away from weakness.

2.9.7 वन्दना

मैं वन्दना करूँ, तुम करुणा करो।
सही रास्ते से कहीं भटक न जाऊँ, ऐसी मुझ पर कृपा करो।।
सुनने को मिलें जब कटु शब्द, सहन करने की देना शक्ति मुझे।
बदले की ना हो कभी भावना, ऐसा विचार बना रहे।।
सदा सेवा में ध्यान रहे, दरिद्रों से प्रेम बना रहे।
शक्ति मेरे में बनी रहे, फल-इच्छा का ना हो ध्यान कभी।।
पूरी हो यह कामना मेरी, ऐसा मुझको दो वरदान।

Prayer
I pray and seek your grace
As in Gayatri-mantra
I seek your grace to keep me on the right path
Give me strength to hear harsh words
May I remain steadfast to Gandhian Ahimsa
May Seva-yoga be my path
May I feel one-ness with the poor
May I always remain engaged in Nishkama-karma.

2.9.8 हे व्याकुल मन मेरे

हे व्याकुल मन मेरे, क्या कहकर धीरज दूँ, कौन से शब्दों से मन शान्त करूँ।
न कोई बाहर है शत्रु खड़ा, न कोई है सता रहा, मन तू ही अन्दर बाहर है।।
जब-जब तू कमज़ोर हुआ, शत्रुओं ने चारों ओर है डेरा डाला, मुझे है छिन्न किया।
ज्योंही शांति अन्दर आई, चारों ओर मित्र दिए दिखाई, सारी विपदा दूर हुई।।
हम अपना मन मज़बूत करें, अन्दर, बाहर सब जगह है रूप तुम्हारा, व्याकुलता की बात नहीं।

Uneasy Mind

What should I do and how should I give peace to my uneasy mind
Everywhere I find myself alone, there is no friend anywhere, everybody is hurting me
When I am weak, it looks as if enemies have surrounded me from all sides
As soon as I become strong, I find friends all around me, all the difficulties vanished
I should not lose heart, keep strong; You are not lonely. His presence is everywhere.

2.9.9 आपत्ति के समय

दुःख का पहाड़ जब टूट पड़ा, मैं खो गई निज सपनों में।
खिड़की के कोने-कोने से झाँका, कहीं उजाला नज़र न आता था।।
मित्रों के घर जाकर देखा, रिश्तों के उलाहने बहुत सहे।
किसी के शब्दों से नहीं मिली सांत्वना, अशान्त हृदय बना रहा।।
गहरी खोज करी अन्दर, बैठा था प्रभु मेरे भीतर।
बोला-मेरे से कर मन की बातें, द्वार खुला है, आगे बढ़कर देख।।

In Times of Difficulty

The time when I was surrounded with deep difficulties, I got completely lost
Looking around in every way; couldn't find any outlet
I visited my friends and relatives, no solution turned out; actually more pain
No words could console me; I was in pain continuously

I took a deep breath; found God inside myself
He said, come forward, express yourself to me
Try, my doors are always open.

2.9.10 घट-घट में भगवान्

घट-घट में है वास तुम्हारा, हर-प्राणी को जीवन-दान दिया।
उदाहरण देकर अपना सतत-कर्म करना सिखलाया और कराया।।
दान की महिमा तभी है ऊँची, जितना लिया उससे अधिक कर्ज़ चुकाया
प्रतिदिन आँखों की ज्योति क्षीण हुई, कमर भी है झुकी हुई।।
समय हाथ से कहीं निकल न जाए, सीमा है समय की बनी हुई।
भगवान भरोसा दो हमें, समय से अपना कर्त्तव्य पूर्ण करें।।

Prayer to God

You are everywhere, pervasive. Giving life to every living being
By giving your own example, you taught everyone how to act in life
Charity means, whatever we get we give more in return
Now my eyesight has become weak, strength is low
Time is running out, it will not wait for me
Oh God! Give me confidence, that I may finish my duties in time.

2.9.11 हृदय की सोच

कभी एकान्त में बैठ अकेले, ध्यान मुझे आ जाता है।
ख़ाली हाथ चले आए थे, पीछे क्या छोड़कर जाएँगे।।
उत्तर अंतःकरण से मुझको आता, सोच न कर कभी इन बातों पर।
सबके सुख-सुविधा की रख सोच हृदय में, काम में बस जुटी रहो।।
बाक़ी निर्णय मुझपर छोड़ो, मुझको सबका है ध्यान बना।
मेरा नाम है "अंतर्यामी", मुझसे कुछ भी नहीं छिपा।।

Inner Thoughts

Sometimes I realize when I sit alone
I came empty-handed, what am I going to leave behind?
Answer came from inside, all this is useless
Think of the good of others; work hard
Result is not in your hand; leave it on me (God)

I take care of everybody; my seat is inside the heart.

2.9.12 सेवा धर्म ही प्रभु का आदेश

जटिल प्रश्न मन में उठता—कौन हूँ? कहाँ से आई? क्या किया? कहाँ जाने की तैयारी है?
इसी उधेड़-बुन में कहीं समय निकल न जाए, फिर पछताना पड़ जाएगा।।
सोच सोचकर क़दम उठाए, सही पड़े या टेढ़े, इसका निर्णय कौन करे।
अन्दर से जो आवाज़ थी आई, उसी सहारे आगे बढ़ते चले गए।।
अब तो पैर भी थक गए, क्या जाकर उत्तर दूँगी, सोच रही थी मन ही मन।
सहसा मुझे, दिया सुनाई - "मैंने जो आदेश दिया!
बस जुटी रहो सदा काम में, यह ही धर्म तुम्हारा है"।।

Message of Seva-Dharma

Question comes to my mind—Who am I? What have I done? Where will I go?
If I brood on this the time will slip, I might have to repent
I thought very carefully, still I do not know whether I did right or wrong
My guide is sitting inside, I went forward intuitively
All of a sudden I heard - "Don't worry, you have done your duty nicely!
Your greatest religion is - do your duty with pure mind and hard work."
Realizing it, I found myself at great peace.

2.9.13 क़दम हमारे, फ़ैसला उसका

सोच-सोच कर क़दम उठाए, सही पड़े या ग़लत पड़े, इसका निर्णय कौन करे।
समय जब हित में होता, सब सही नज़र आता है, सारे पाँसे सीधे पड़ते हैं।।
मन में किसी तरह का स्वार्थ न हो, फल की इच्छा का ध्यान नहीं।
जो कुछ हुआ, हो रहा है, आगे होने वाला है, कुंजी उसके हाथ में है।।
संतोष हमें बस करना है, जो कुछ किया स्वार्थ रहित किया, और रखा मन में परहित-भाव।

We Go Forward, Decision is of God

We put forward every step after deep thinking, who knows they are right or wrong

When the time is in our favor, every step turns out correct
Keeping no selfish desire and no desire of fruits, did our duty
Whatever is happening and what results we are going to get, it is in God's hand
We have to be satisfied, done everything with selfless thoughts and for the good of all.

2.9.14 कलियुग में प्रार्थना

सभ्यता की आड़ में जब उल्लू सीधा किया जाता हो, तब तुम रक्षा करना।
झूठ बोलने वाले को चतुर कहकर नारा दिया जाय, तब विवेक का रास्ता दिखाना।।
निरपराधी को जब प्रतारणा और कष्ट झेलने पड़ें, तब सहन करने की शक्ति देना।
कठिन से कठिन आपत्ति में जब हँसी उड़ाई जाती हो, तब तुम धीरज सिखाना।।

Prayer in the Present Time

Oh God! Help the innocent who are harassed, by the so-called cultured gang
Give right thinking to those who are tamasika and anti-social
When faultless people are blamed and criticized, please teach patience
In most difficult times, when people make fun of us,
Show us the way of forbearance.

2.9.15 कलाकार

उस कलाकार को देखो, जिसने रचा ये जगत महान्।
सूरज, चाँद, सितारे चमके, पहाड़, नदियाँ, झरने बहते।।
हर फूल और पत्ते निराले, मन मोहित करने वाले।
पक्षीगण आकाश में डोलें, मानव-गण पृथ्वी पर विचरें।।
कोई दो कृति एक समान नहीं, फिर भी संतुलन की कमी नहीं।
अनेक में एकता बनी हुई, साधना कितनी है सधी सुई।।
इसको सदा बनाए रखो, महान् कलाकार से शिक्षा लो।

Creator

Pray to the Almighty who has created this Universe
Sun, Moon, Stars, Mountains, Rivers, Brooks are all his creation

Trees, flowers, leaves and creepers are all so beautiful
Birds fly in the sky and human beings walk on the earth
No two things are alike, even then we observe balance
There is unity in diversity, what a remarkable pattern we see
We must maintain the beauty of His creation, by following His teachings.

2.9.16 मुझे भरोसा तेरा है

एक-एक कर लौकिक भरोसे टूट रहे, मुझे भरोसा तेरा है।
दुनिया में जब आई थी, अनजान थी, भोली-भाली थी।।
अपना पराया नहीं था कोई, तेरी कृपा से बड़ी हुई।
माता-पिता के रूप में लौकिक सम्बन्ध जो यहाँ बने, धीरे-धीरे सब हैं छूट रहे।।
तेरा सम्बन्ध सदा बना रहा, दिन प्रतिदिन बढ़ता चला गया।
कैसी भी कोई आपत्ति आई, तेरे सहारे पार हुई।
कभी किसी बात का भय न मुझे हुआ, मुझे भरोसा तेरा था।।
आज इस जीवन की संध्या में, खड़ी हूँ, हिम्मत है। मुझे भरोसा तेरा है।
क्या डर है किसी बात का उसको, जिसे भरोसा तेरा है।।

In God We Trust

God has always protected me
The Vedas have declared - "Matridevo bhava"
God took the form of my mother
The Vedas continued—"Pitridevo bhava"
God took the form of my father
"Acharyadevo bhava"—God took the form of my teachers
My Antaryami God has protected me at every moment
I hear the words in my heart
"Be not afraid - I am looking after you"

2.9.17 सब को सम्मति दे भगवान्

हे भगवान्! तेरा नाम है दाता, तू सबके हृदय में है बसा हुआ।
तू पालन हारा है, सब पर दया-दृष्टि बरसाने वाला है।।
एक समान समझ रहा सभी को, परस्पर भाव की शिक्षा देता है सब को।
फिर मानव क्यूँ अपना अस्तित्व है भूल रहा, जुटा जा रहा है विनाश करने में।।
सता रहा है एक-एक को, देश-देश का बना है दुश्मन।

साइंस ने की है बड़ी तरक़्क़ी, नई-नई निकाली हैं खोज।।
सुलझाने को सभी समस्याएँ और बढ़ जाने को पूर्णता की ओर।
ईश्वर करो कृपा ऐसी हम पर
सुलझ जाएँ समस्याएँ भाई-चारे से।।
तेरी सीख सदा रहे ध्यान में
बढ़ते चलें शांति, विकास की ओर।।

God Grant us Peace

God, you are the provider, you are residing in our hearts
The care giver, you teach us how to care, how to have empathy and compassion
You teach us equality, how to be just
Our egoism is only a path to sure destruction
Even the discoveries of science
Can not be compared to Your grace
In helping solve the world's problems of hunger, poverty and conflict
We bow to your grace and your teachings
May they grant us peace.

2.9.18 गायत्री मंत्र की प्रार्थना

गांधीजी की प्रार्थना सभा में -
रामधुन का गान होता था -
सबको सम्मति दे भगवान्!
यह गायत्री मंत्र का सरल रूप था।
धियो यो नः प्रचोदयात्
अर्थात्, हे प्रभु! सब को सदबुद्धी दो।
यह प्रार्थना विश्व शान्ति की प्रार्थना है।।
संसार में लड़ाई-झगड़ा बन्द कैसे हो?
जो काम हमारी शक्ति से पूरा नहीं हो सकता।
उसके लिए गांधी जी रोज़ प्रभु से प्रार्थना करते थे।।
गायत्री मंत्र के सहारे।।

The Prayer of Gayatri Mantra

Gandhiji used to pray using the Gayatri mantra's Hindi version

In his gatherings on a daily basis
Praying for good thoughts and wisdom to all
This prayer is central for today's world
Ravaged by war, conflict, natural disasters and world hun
Whatever is outside our capacity to complete
We pray to you O God!
Please give us good thoughts and wisdom
So we may choose the path of peace.

CHAPTER 2.10

Nature is the Great Teacher

(प्रकृति से शिक्षा लो)

2.10.1 प्रकृति से शिक्षा लो

सूरज, चाँद, सितारे, पहाड़ नदियाँ, फूल निराले।
उदाहरण देके अपना, कह रहे हैं बारम्बार।।
क्षणिक अवकाश नहीं है उनको, जो निरन्तर कर्म में लीन।
पहाड़ और नदियों को देखो, हरा भरा करते धरती को।।
समस्त प्राणियों को भोजन देते, स्वयं सर्दी-गर्मी में तपते हैं।
जगत का पालन ध्येय है उनका, नहीं दूसरा कोई ध्यान।।
इन पेड़ों को देखो, ऋषि मुनि से लगते हैं।
आँधी तूफ़ानों से लड़कर, सबको छाया देते हैं।।
ज्ञान इन्हीं से सीखें हम, जो सबको गले लगाते हैं।

Nature is the Great Teacher

Sun, moon and stars, mountains, rivers and flowers
Are all teaching us by their example
They take no pause and are continuously busy in action
Look at these mountains and rivers, they keep the earth fertile and green
They provide food for everyone and keep them alive
Look at these trees, they look like saints and sages
They give shelter to all
Be active and help everyone-this is what we learn from Nature.

2.10.2 प्रकृति का संदेश

प्रात समय लालिमा आकाश में छाई हुई थी, पक्षी एक पंक्ति में उड़े जा रहे थे।
पुकार रहे थे एक दूसरे को, कोई पीछे छूट न जाए, एक से एक थे जुड़े हुए।।

निगाह गई फिर बगिया पर, पत्तों पर ओस की बूँदें नाच रही थीं।
कह रही थीं, कर्म की लगन है हमको, सेवा के लिए हम हैं व्याकुल।।
आँखों को कर रहीं थी मुग्ध, त्याग का दे रहीं थी संदेश।
त्याग, संयम को देख सभी के, मन हुआ प्रसन्न और शांति प्राप्त हुई।।

Message from Nature
It was blissful dawn, sky was red, birds were flying in a line
They were calling each other, they were afraid no one should be left behind
Afterwards I saw drops of dew, as if they were dancing on the blades of grass
Lovely flowers were blossoming, herbs were smelling fragrant
They were anxious to provide service to others, only demanding little water in return
All were giving the message of sacrifice
And discipline, making everybody happy.

2.10.3 प्रकृति से सीखो
झरने हों या नदियाँ नाले हों, सब अविरल गति से बहते रहते हैं।
पथ में कितने रोड़े, पत्थर हों, क्या कोई इनको है रोक सका?
प्रकृति ही सब कुछ है, वह ही ज्ञान सिखाती, आगे ले जाती है।
जीवन में कैसी भी आपत्ति आए, उसको पार करो, डरो नहीं।।
प्रेरणा ईश्वर से मिलती, सबक़ प्रकृति से मिलता है।

Learn from Nature
Brooks, streams and rivers all flow with continuous pace
In spite of many stones and pebbles in their way
No matter how many difficulties they face, nobody can stop them
Nature is everything, it teaches you and takes you forward
No matter how many difficulties you face in life, just cross them; have no fear in your heart
We get inspiration from God, and nature helps us to learn the lessons of life.

2.10.4 कच्ची टहनी
मैं पेड़ की कच्ची टहनी हूँ, मुझे न सताओ किसी तरह।
छोटी थी फूलों से लदी हुई, सभी देख प्रसन्नता पाते थे।।

बड़ी हुई, फल लगे चारों ओर, मेरे से सबकी भूख मिटी।
सेवा करते-करते झुक गई हूँ, अन्दर से अब भी हूँ मज़बूत।।
सूखी टहनी किस काम की है, तोड़ा और जला दिया।
जब तक सबके आई काम, सदा हरी बनी रही।।

Delicate Branch

I am a delicate branch don't hurt me in any way
When I was young, I was full of flowers, everybody was happy to see me
At the time of maturity, was full of fruits, people used to satisfy their hunger by feeding on me
Now I am old and tired serving all; but I am still strong from inside
Dry branch is useless; people break it and burn it
I was always green and fresh and very useful for others.

2.10.5 अविरल कर्म

आँख खुली, किरण सूर्य की, खिड़की से थी झाँक रही।
बार-बार कह रही थी मुझसे, तुम भी मेरे साथ चलो।।
मैं करती काम निरन्तर, देती हूँ यह ज्ञान तुम्हें।
धरती ने है धान की चादर ओढ़ी, फूलों से ख़ूब सजाई है।।
करो नियमित काम सदा, हर्षित और उल्लास हृदय से।
सफल होगा जीवन तुम्हारा, कर सबके काम लगन से।।

Work Without Break

I got up and saw sunshine through the window
I felt as if it was telling me - come along and move with me
Continuously I work, I want to give you that knowledge
Look, the fields are green and are decorated with flowers
We must work continuously with a happy heart
This is the key to success, work hard for all.

2.10.6 गुलाब

गुलाब, तेरे गुणों से तेरी महानता, सुन्दरता है तेरा ताज।
कष्टों में तू पला हुआ, निखर कर बना फूल गुलाब।।
धागे में तू गया पिरोया, भगवान के गले का बना हार।

पंखड़ियाँ पूजा की थाली में विराज रहीं, कर रहीं स्वागत वीरों का।।
काँटों से तू डरा नहीं, बाधाओं के बीच रहकर, कोमलता सदा बनी रही।
तेरे से शिक्षा मिली सभी को, त्याग, तपस्या सेवा की।।

Rose
Oh Rose! You are so great and beautiful because of your great qualities
You lived in immense difficulties and finally became such a beautiful rose
People made garlands of you and put around the neck of God's images
Your petals are being put in the plate to welcome heroes
You have no fear of thorns, living in all the difficulties, still you maintain your softness
We all learn from you of sacrifice, resilience in hardships and service.

2.10.7 पतझड़ में सुनहरी किरणें

पतझड़ में सुनहरी किरणें, छिटक रही हैं पत्ते पत्ते पर।
कहीं दिखाई देती लाल, कहीं पीली और कहीं हरी दिखाई देती हैं।।
हे किरण, तेरा कोई रंग नहीं, या फिर सारे रंग भरे हैं तेरे में।
तेरा रंग रूप बदलता नहीं दिखाई देता, हमें क्यूँ इतना असमंजस में डाला है।।
तू कह रही है, मैं शान्त हूँ, बाहर से मत परखो मुझको।
जिस रूप में जो मुझे देख रहा, उसी रूप में मैं दिखाई देती हूँ।।

Autumn's Beauty
In fall, Sun's rays are truly wonderful and very beautiful
Golden rays of Sun are falling on each leaf
Still some look red, some look yellow, and some look green
It is as if they have no color, or that all the colors are hidden inside
We are not able to imagine all the different colors that appear, and are astonished
Perhaps they are saying to us, "Do not try to see only what you can see,
I will appear the way that you can imagine me!"

2.10.8 रात की रानी

रात अंधेरी, घना था जंगल, पानी था बरस रहा।
मैं खड़ी अकेली, आँधी, तूफ़ान के सहन थपेड़े, महक रही थी।।
मेरी तरह नहीं कोई था दूजा, मैं तो "रात की रानी" थी।
स्वतन्त्रता थी, खुशी मेरी बनी हुई थी, सबको सुगन्ध पहुँचाती थी।।
रूप मेरा ऐसा था, जैसे 'आकाश गंगा' धरती पर उतरी हो।
मैं तो सेवा में जुटी हुई थी, स्वतः जीव आकर्षित होता था।।
बिन बुलाए पास थे आते, मन मेरा हर्षित होता था।
इसीलिए नाम पड़ा मेरा 'रात की रानी' वातावरण सुगन्धित करने वाली।।

Queen of the Night

Dark night, thick forest, heavy rain everywhere
While standing alone, tolerating storm, I exude fragrance
No one was like me; I was a nightingale, queen of the night
Independent I was, and I was happy, giving lovely aroma to others
My beauty was such, as if the milky-way had descended on earth
While serving others in silence thus, I would attract everyone
Even without calling, all came to me. I felt happy at heart
My qualities made me queen of the night
Lovely fragrance was all around.

2.10.9 जीवन संगीत है

जीवन जीना उसी ने सीखा, जिसके जीवन में संगीत भरा।
यह नहीं है आता पुस्तक से, नहीं है आता सीख सिखाने से।।
इसका सीधा सम्बन्ध जुड़ा हुआ है प्रकृति से एवं ब्रह्म-ज्ञान से।
अंतर्ज्योति पनपती है, प्रकट होती है कर्मों के करने में।।
स्वयं को शीतलता देती है, सभी को एक बनाती है।
ईश्वर का रूप है प्रकृति, संगीत है मानव का सच्चा रूप।।

Life is Music

Learn from one who knows how to live with life full of music
This is not learnt from books or reading
But is connected directly with love of Nature and knowledge of Brahman

Intuitive understanding of this comes from the quality of your actions
Giving you peace in your mind and unity with all life
The reality of human beings is reflected in the music of life
The way Nature is the reflection of Brahman.

2.10.10 गिलहरी की सीख
निगाह गई, पेड़ पर देखा, गिलहरी फुदक-फुदक कर खेल रही थीं।
बीन रहीं थीं कुछ धरती पर, एक दूसरे की भूख मिटाने को।।
कितना सच्चा प्यार था उनमें, होड़ का तो नाम नहीं था।
देख उनका प्यार परस्पर, कितना मन को सन्तोष हुआ।।
त्याग-प्रेम की महिमा ऐसी, जिसका कोई पारावार नहीं।

Lessons from a Squirrel
Looking outside, the squirrels were playing up and down near the tree
Some were picking up the seeds to fulfill their hunger
There was no competition, only love for each other
My heart was full of peace and happiness when I saw so much love and cooperation
We cannot compare this type of love and sacrifice with artificial affection.

2.10.11 बदलता जीवन
समय-चक्र निराला है, अदलता है, बदलता, इसको बस स्वीकार करो।
यह किसी के हाथ नहीं, और नहीं किसी की दौलत पूँजी है।।
फूल पत्ते सभी सूख गए, झाड़ियाँ सूखी हैं पड़ी हुई।
जीव आया, चला गया, कहाँ से आया, कहाँ गया, इसका किसी को पता नहीं।।
एक बात समझ में आती है, एक के जाने पर ही दूसरे का जन्म हुआ करता है।
प्रकृति का नियम यही, उस पर किसी का अधिकार नहीं, यह ईश्वर की माया है।।

Changes Always Come in Life
Time goes on changing, no one has any control over it. Accept it!
It is not our personal property, it is related with God

Look at these dry flowers and leaves, bushes and grass
Life comes and goes
One thing it teaches us
New life comes after the decay of old life
This is the rule of Nature.

2.10.12 प्रकृति से लो शिक्षा

प्रत्येक रात्रि आकाश में ये नक्षत्र, चाँद, सितारे, अपनी कथा सुनाते हैं।
परस्पर भाव और आकर्षण में है अस्तित्व हमारा, इसी सहारे हैं टिके हुए।।
संयम से रहते हैं और धरती को जगमग करते हैं, निर्भर हैं सब एक दूसरे पर।
सूरज को देखो, बादल को देखो, करते अपना काम निरन्तर।।
इनके भरोसे हम सब जीवित हैं, करते धरती को उपजाऊ हैं।
ये प्रकृति की हरियाली, पहाड़, समुद्र और झरने, सभी लगे हुए हैं देने में।।
स्वार्थ का तो नाम नहीं, शांत हैं, त्याग भावना पर रहते हैं।
प्रकृति हमें दे रही शिक्षा।
परस्पर और त्याग भाव से सब जुड़े रहो।।

Learn Paraspara-Bhava from Nature

Lord Krishna says in Gita - I taught yoga to the Sun
The sun created life on earth, giving heat and light
Clouds give us water
The sun, moon, and stars
All are rotating in a perfectly co-ordinated manner
Mutual co-ordination and help is Paraspara-Bhava
Gita says - Paraspara-Bhava is essential for good-of-all
Mother Nature is our great teacher.

CHAPTER 2.11

Childhood Memories

(बचपन के संस्कार, पुरानी यादें)

2.11.1 बचपन की याद

स्वतन्त्रता संग्राम देखा मैंने, स्वतन्त्र भारत देखा मैंने।
स्वतन्त्रता में पली हुई, स्वतन्त्रता से की पढ़ाई।।
मैं क्या जानूँ ऊँच-नीच, जाति-पाँति, धनी-निर्धन।
एकता, समानता का लेकर नारा मैंने जीना सीखा था।।
इन्हीं बातों को करके याद मैं भारत का करती ध्यान।
कहते हैं! पुरानी बातें भूल जाओ, क्यों भूलूँ अपना सुन्दर बचपन।।

Childhood Memory

I saw freedom fight and later I saw free India
I studied and grew in that atmosphere of freedom
In that atmosphere I learnt only equality
I never used to care who is rich and who is poor, equality and oneness were the motto
Caste and creed were out of question
Unity and equality were the slogans of children, youth and old
I remember those days with great fondness, this was our country India
How can I forget my past, my childhood was very rich and full of life.

2.11.2 मेरा जन्म और बचपन

स्वतन्त्रता-सैनानी, देश-भक्त, सन् इकत्तीस में मेरे पिता बरेली जेल गए।
माता, ताई-ताऊजी के पास गई, जो बरेली में थे बसे हुए।।

उनके सान्निध्य में मेरा जन्म हुआ और उनको मुझसे प्यार हुआ।
कुछ वर्षों बाद, सात साल की आयु में, ताई-ताऊजी का प्यार ले गया फिर उनके पास।।
तीन साल इलाहाबाद में उनके पास रही, वहीं पड़ी नींव कला की और पढ़ाई की।
बड़ी बहन स्वर्ण मुझे बड़े प्रेम से भिन्न-भिन्न कला सिखातीं और ज्ञान की बातें करतीं।।
मैं भी उनसे ऐसी चिपटी, जैसे एक बाप की दो बेटी।
भूल नहीं सकती अपना बचपन, बड़ी गहरी छाप पड़ी मन पर।।

My Childhood

My father was a freedom-fighter, great patriot, went to Bareilly jail in 1931
Mother went to Bareilly, with my uncle and aunt, who were posted there
I was born there.
They became very fond of me.
They took me to Allahabad from Muzaffarnagar when I was seven.
I stayed with them for three years. I got my early education and training in art
My elder sister Swarna, taught me handwork and used to tell me stories
I became so fond of her, she was more than a real sister to me
I can not forget my childhood
It was very rich, full of memories.

2.11.3 सच्ची पहचान

भिन्नता है हर वृक्ष और हर पौधे में, जैसे हैं बीज पड़े, वैसा हुआ आकार।
जैसे बचपन में संस्कार पड़े, वैसा हुआ उसका व्यवहार।।
मनुष्य की पहचान उसी से होती, जो हैं उसके संगी-साथी।
धन-दौलत, शान-ठान, झूठी बातें, ये हैं केवल आडंबर।।
यह सब दो दिन की माया है, नहीं सच्ची है पहचान।

सीधी, सच्ची, सरल सोच ही है, अपना सही रूप और आकार।।

What is Reality?

No two things are alike, every tree and sapling is different
Depending on the seed
Whatever impressions we gather in our childhood, we act accordingly afterwards
People are recognized correctly by the company of their friends
Money and show-off, these are all shallow and false
They are not the reality, they are not the truth
Truth, simplicity, and straight-forwardness
Are the real qualities that pay in life.

2.11.4 कला

कला है मेरी संगी साथी, हृदय-कुंज की है पटरानी।
सदा मेरे साथ है रहती, नए ढंग से, सुचारू रूप से, काम कराती, मन बहलाती है।।
अकेलापन कभी न होने देती, मन-मस्तिष्क में सदा है बसती।
हर समय नए विचारों को लाती, हाथों से कला खूब कराती।।
मैं इसकी बड़ी आभारी हूँ, सीधा विधाता से इसका नाता है।
भीतर होती इसकी सोच, बाहर होता मन-मोहक रूप।।
जितना इससे किया प्रेम, उतना ही जीवन में बरसा।
सुख, शांति और प्रेम।।

Art

Art is queen of my heart and a permanent companion
Your continued presence teaches me new ways of doing things and makes me always happy
I never feel lonely, your presence is always in my heart and mind
Always you give me new thoughts and they make me creative
I am grateful to you, it is directly related to my inner self
Everything comes from inside, only the reflection is outside
More I love you, more peace, happiness and attachment I get.

2.11.5 जीवन ही भाषा है

मेरा जीवन मेरी भाषा, दोनों में कुछ भेद नहीं।
मेरा हँसना-बोलना, चलना-फिरना या अपने निज-कामों को करना।।
मेरे जीवन की कथा यही, मेरी यही निशानी है।
यथासमय सबको भोजन देकर, संग बैठकर खाना-पीना।
इसको समझो सेवा-भाव मेरा, इसका मुझको शौक़ बड़ा।।
जो कुछ ज्ञान-शौक़ मिला ईश्वर से, उसको सदा विस्तृत करना।
यह सोच मेरी बड़ी पुरानी है, यह मेरी अपनी कहानी है।।
आज जो भी मैं हूँ उसमें सबका सहयोग निरन्तर।
हृदय से है सबको धन्यवाद मेरा, सबको है प्यार मेरा।।

Life Lived as Language

My life is my language; there is no difference between the two
My laughter, words, moving around, or my daily tasks
They are the story of my life, and they mark my life
By giving food to others at the right occasion; eating together
Consider this as my offering of service to others, and my joy
Whatever knowledge I have gained from God, I like to pass on to others through my actions and my words
This is my age-old personal hobby and this is my life story
Whatever I am today is a result of everyone's contribution
I am grateful to everyone from the bottom of my heart, and I give my love to everyone.

2.11.6 भारत के आदर्श

भारत ऋषि-मुनियों की नगरी कहलाती है, इसकी संस्कृति, इतिहास महान है।
राम, कृष्ण, बुद्ध जैसे अवतार हुए, सीता, सावित्री, शकुन्तला जैसी त्यागी दयावान ज्ञानी नारी हुईं।।
संस्कृति इतनी ऊँची, 'महाभारत', 'गीता-अनुगीता' जैसे ग्रन्थ लिखे गए और पढ़े गए।
लक्ष्मी बाई, वीर शिवाजी ने क्या कभी किसी से हार थी मानी।।
गाँधी जैसे नेता ने, हथियार रहित, ब्रिटिश-सत्ता को ललकार दिया।
कभी किसी देश पर किया न हमला, जो आया, प्रेम से उसको बसा लिया।।

इसके आदर्शों से लें हम शिक्षा, रक्षा करना धर्म हमारा।
मैंने यह सीखा बचपन में याद रहेगा जीवन-भर।।

Indian Ideals

History and ideals of India are great, it is a country of great sages and saints
Rama, Krishna and Buddha were incarnations of God
Women like Sita, Savitri and Shakuntala were very kind, helpful and knowledgeable
India produced big scriptures like the Geeta and AnuGita
Bravery of Shivaji and Lakshmi Bai is well known in Indian history
A hero like Gandhi turned out British empire without any violence
India never attacked any country and accepted anyone who came to her
We must protect these ideals and should get inspiration from them
I learnt this in my childhood and it will never be forgotten.

2.11.7 बदलती परिभाषा

इस लम्बी आयु में हर चीज़ बदलती देखी है, परिभाषा है बदल गई।
विद्या का प्रतिदिन हो रहा विकास, परिभाषा उसकी भी बदली है।।
अहंकार की नहीं है सीमा, बच्चे, बूढ़े और युवक में है भारी भेद हुआ।
श्री अरविन्द ने दिव्य-चक्षु से देखा भविष्य का रूप और कहा -
परिभाषा फिर बदलेगी।।
और विश्व में फिर से सात्त्विक वृत्ति होगी विकसित।

Definitions have Changed

In 85 years of my life, the definition of everything has changed
Knowledge is expanding, but its definition is also changing
There is no limit of arrogance, old and young are being considered equal in every way
Sri Aurobindo's divine eyes helped him foretell the future
He said, "Definitions will change again,
And mankind will move towards righteousness."

2.11.8 अमेरिका में पहली पीढ़ी

कथा सुनो उन भारतीयों की, जो अमेरिका में पहली पीढ़ी के कहलाते हैं।
परिश्रमी थे, त्याग था, जोश था रग-रग में, कुछ कर जाने की इच्छा लेकर आए थे।।
जो भी पूँजी पास थी उनके, सँभल-कर खर्ची थी, कुछ अपने ऊपर, रोज़ सन्तान के आए वो काम।
स्वयं ने किया अथक परिश्रम, धन लगाया बच्चों पर, सफल जीवन की इच्छा थी।।
किन्तु व्यर्थ नहीं हुआ उनका त्याग।
उनके ज्वलन्त उदाहरण से प्रेरित होकर-
नई पीढ़ी ने अपनी कर्मभूमि की सेवा की।
और अपनी ईश्वर-प्रदत्त प्रतिभा के कारण पाया सम्मान।।

First Generation of Indians in America

Listen to the story of first generation of Indians who came to America
They were hard-working, ready to sacrifice, full of enthusiasm, and had a desire to achieve something worthwhile
Whatever small money they had, spent carefully, some on themselves and saved some to use for children
Continuously they were busy, money was spent on children, keeping the idea of success in mind
But their sacrifice did not go in vain
They laid the foundation, setting an example for the new generation
And the three million Indians have made a name making their contributions.

2.11.9 प्रभु से प्राप्त वृत्ति

मुझे न चाहिए रुपया-पैसा, मुझे न चाहिए राज-महल।
सिनेमा घर हों, या फिर बड़े-बड़े होटल हों, मुझे नहीं आकर्षित करते।।
मुझ को मुझमें रहने दो, झूठे दबाव की करो न इच्छा।
जो कुछ कला भगवान ने दी है मुझको, उसको ही बढ़ने दो।।
मेरा वास्तिवक रूप यही है, वही दिशा मुझको भाती है।
ज्ञान नहीं बाहर से मिलता, वह अन्दर की सोच हमारी है।।

God-Given Aptitude

I don't care for money, nor do I care for palatial buildings
All these theaters and big hotels do not attract me
Do not try to impress me with false notions, leave me the way I am
Whatever qualities I got from God, let them develop
That is my reality, that is what I like
True knowledge never comes from outside, it is what we think inside

2.11.10 मजबूरी

मजबूरी, तुझसे मेरी मित्रता गहरी, हर समय मेरे साथ है रहती।
सबसे बड़ी शिक्षक है मेरी, हर मोड़ पर आ खड़ी है होती, सफल जीवन की कला सिखाती।।
जैसे ही कोई आपत्ति आन पड़ी, दिया धक्का तुझको, झेल समस्या आगे बढ़ जाती।
सहन शक्ति है तुझमें, मेरा पीछा कभी न छोड़ती, अन्य किसी रूप में आ मुझे पकड़ती।।
साथ तेरा कभी न छोड़ूँगी, सीख ले समझौता करना, मान ले कहना मेरा।
मुझमें हिम्मत है आती, जूझने की, बढ़ने की, सहन करने की और आगे बढ़ जाने की।।
ऐहसान तेरा है मुझपर भारी, प्रयत्न करूँगी सदा निभाने की।

Limitation

Limitation! You and I are great friends, we always live together
You are my biggest teacher. At any time of difficulty you teach me how to overcome
Whenever I face problems, I push you and move forward
You never leave me alone, follow me all the time and catch hold of me in whatever way you can
I feel you are saying as if I have to compromise with you
I got confidence to face, to fight, to push myself to go ahead
You oblige me a lot and I will also try to fulfill my obligation.

2.11.11 कहानी मेरी

चेहरे की झुर्रियाँ हुई हैं गहरी, हाथों की स्थिरता कमज़ोर पड़ी।

चाल पड़ गई है धीमी, स्मृति भी हो गई है हल्की।।
कम हुई शारीरिक शक्ति, अनुभव की गाथा लम्बी और हुई।
हर मुद्रा और हर कर्म मेरे सुना रहे हैं कहानी मेरी।।
कैसी सोच रही जीवन में, कैसा व्यवहार सबके संग किया।
यह कहने की कोई बात नहीं, सब कुछ लिखा है चेहरे पर।।
हर मुद्रा प्रकट करती है भाव मेरा, हर शब्द कह रहा कहानी मेरी।

My Story

Now my hands are not stable and my face has wrinkles
I walk slowly and my memory has become weak
Physically I am weaker but my experiences are very long
Every action and reflection is telling my life story
How I used to act and how I used to think and behave all along
Everything is written on my face, I need not tell
My way of life and thoughts are my reality.

2.11.12 शांतिपर्व की देन

मुझे न चाहिए रुपया-पैसा, मुझे न चाहिए शान और शौक़त।
सब कुछ पड़ा दे रहा दिखाई, फिर भी हल चल मन में है बनी हुई।।
आज समाज बना है एकांगी, भरोसा प्रभु पर करना है।
अंतर्यामी का मिला संदेश -
याद कर शांति पर्व को -
ज़रा सोच—भीष्म-पितामह कितने कष्ट में थे।
जब दिया उन्होंने शांतिपर्व का महान् उपदेश?

Inspiration from Shanti-Parva

I do not much value wealth, nor glamour and show
I see everything all around, but my mind is not at ease
Society has become so individualistic that everyone has to depend on God
I heard inspiring message of Almighty—
Think of Shanti-Parva—
What was Bhisma-Pitamaha's physical condition
When he gave to Yudhisthira unparalleled teaching?

2.11.13 आशा अभिलाषा

कहते हैं—छोड़, सभी आशा को अधिकारों को। ये सब दुःख के साधन हैं।
मेरी तो अभिलाषा और प्रबल हुई, क्यों छोड़ चलूँ अपनी इच्छित-आशा को।।
समय अवश्य थोड़ा है, सिर सदा झुका रहे, आँखों में प्रेम झलकता हो।
मुँह पर मुसकान बनी रहे, मुख से निकलें हित के बोल सदा।।
हृदय में प्यार भरा हो मेरे, मन में सीधी सोच रहे।
हाथ बढ़ें सबकी सेवा को, पैर सबके संग चलें।।
भगवन् ! मेरी अभिलाषा पूर्ण करो, मिले ऐसा आशीर्वाद मुझे।

Desire and Expectation

People say—let go of all your desires and feelings of entitlement behind; they can only bring unhappiness
But my longing has become more awakened; why should I leave my true desires behind?
Time might be limited for me, but my head should always be bowed, and my eyes should always reflect love for others
My face should always be lit with a smile, and my words should always be sweet
My heart should always be full of love. My thoughts should always be pure
My arms should always be extended in service, and I should walk in unity with others
O God, please fulfill my desires and give me your blessings

CHAPTER 2.12

Heart-Felt Feelings on Special Occasions

(स्मरणीय अवसरों पर श्रद्धाप्रेरित उद्‌गार)

2.12.1 दीपावली

दीपावली के इस महान-पर्व पर, मन्दिर में है भीड़ जमी।
सभी मस्त हैं लिए हाथ में माला, लिए आरती का थाल।।
मुझे तो इस अवसर पर, गाँधी हर समय दिखाई देते हैं।
तीसरे दर्जे के डिब्बे से उतरते, गले में माला पहनाई थी।।
वे अब भी मुझको दर्शन देते, बातें बहुत समझाते हैं।
चिन्ता मत कर मन्दिर जाने की, दरिद्रों में भगवान् की मूरत देख।।
भूखे-प्यासे पड़े कुटिया में, परम पिता की सन्तान हैं ये।
तन पर फटे पुराने चीथड़े हैं, खा रहे नमक से रोटी हैं।।
इनकी कर जी जान से सेवा, ईश्वर इनमें है रमा हुआ।
धन-दौलत जो भी है पास तेरे, है सब धरोहर रूप मिली।।
कल किसी औंर की थी, कल किसी और की होने वाली है।
कर सद् उपयोग पैसे-पैसे का, मत समझ इस पर अपना अधिकार।।

Festival of Lights

At the festival of Diwali, temples are full of crowds
Everybody is busy, they are holding garlands or sweets to offer to God
On this occasion, I see Gandhi as I close my eyes for prayer
I recall when I put a garland around his neck
When he descended from the third class compartment of the train

Now when I see him, he advises me to do sewa
Do not worry about going to temple, pay attention to the poor
They have only torn clothes, children are eating bread with salt
Serve them. See God in them.
Worldly belongings that you have, will be with you for a short while only
In the past someone else was the owner, in the future it will be of someone else
Spend your wealth for good causes, your right on money is only for a short period.

2.12.2 विवेकानन्द जयन्ती

हिंदू मंदिर में था विवेकानन्द की पूजा का अवसर।
अधिकतर वक्ताओं ने शिकागो के भाषण का उल्लेख किया।।
हमने कहा—दीर्घ काल तक नया मार्ग दिखलाने वाले चार भाषण।
जो उन्होंने दिये 1896 में 'व्यावहारिक वेदान्त' के नाम से।
1897 में रामकृष्ण मिशन की स्थापना भी हुई।।
व्यावहारिक वेदान्त की पुष्टि के लिए।
अन्य ऋषियों ने फैलाया व्यावहारिक वेदान्त के क्रान्तिकारी विचारों को सारे विश्व में।।
व्यावहारिक वेदान्त का प्रचार ही है स्वामी विवेकानन्द की असली पूजा।

Vivekananda Jayanti

Hindu Mandir celebrated Vivekananda-Jayanti
Most of the speakers highlighted his Chicago lectures
We said—Four lectures that he delivered in 1896,
And which started the Practical Vedanta Movement
Have had a long-lasting impact
Ramakrishna Mission was established in 1897
To keep alive the Practical Vedanta vision
Vedantic revolutionaries strengthened this movement
Which became world famous
Real puja of Swami Vivekananda
Consists in promoting Practical Vedanta.

2.12.3 प्रिय इंदु की पुण्य स्मृति

पचास वर्ष कैसे बीत गए, तुम रोज़ पास खड़े दिखाई देते हो।
कारण हर बात का होता, तुम शीतलता, प्यार, त्याग के देने वाले हो।।
उम्र अवश्य छोटी पाई, काम किए हैं बड़े बड़े, सबकी आँखों के बने हो तारा।
सूर्य से मिली शक्ति, चन्द्रमा से मिली शीतलता, इंदु नाम पड़ा तुम्हारा।।
बच्चा-बच्चा तुमसे चिपटा, बड़ों ने सदा गले लगाया।
अन्त समय में आए देश के काम, कर्त्तव्य खूब निभाया।।
तुम सदा हम सबके पास बसे, अमर रहेगा नाम तुम्हारा, बलिदान तुम्हारा।
तुम्हारी याद में-उर्मिला मौसी, मौसाजी सत्य।।

In Memory of Dear Indu

It is surprising how the 50 years have passed, I see you standing next to me all the time
There is a reason for this, you gave peace, love and message of sacrifice
In spite of your short life, you have done great deeds and have become a shining star in the eyes of everybody
You got strength from sun and peace from moon that made your name Indu
All children loved you a lot, and elders always embraced you
In your last breaths, you gave your life for the country, considering it your duty
You will always live with us: your name and sacrifice will be remembered forever
Remembering you, Urmila Mausi and Mausaji Satya.

2.12.4 आभार

मेरे ताई-ताऊजी, पिताजी-अम्माँ, शारीरिक रूप से बिछुड़ गए।
जब भी उनका ध्यान है आता, कुछ नई ज्ञान की बात सिखाते हैं।।
कितना ऊँचा जीवन था उनका, वे त्याग-पूर्ण बलिदानी थे।
नियमित जीवन, सुन्दर सीख, सात्त्विक भाव, इससे मिली मुझे शिक्षा।।
जो भी मुझ में गुण आए, वे बस उन्हीं के हैं दिए हुए।
कमज़ोरियाँ समस्त मेरी अपनी हैं, चाहती हूँ उनको दूर करूँ।।

Gratefulness

My uncle and aunt, father and mother - have all left me physically

Whenever I think about them, I always feel they are giving me good advice
Their life was full of sacrifice and their character was high
Their disciplined life, right advice, truthful nature
Gave me useful teachings
All the weaknesses are mine
I am grateful to them and I pay my respects.

2.12.5 सर्वहितकारिणी सभा

गीता से सीखा लोकसंग्रह—अर्थात् सर्वहित का संदेश।
मेरे सास-ससुर ने 1920 में -
सर्वहितकारिणी सभा स्थापित की थी।
मैंने 2010 में इस सभा को देखा
90 वर्ष पहले सर्वहित का उदाहरण देने वाले–
प्रेरणा-दायक सास-ससुर को मैंने किया हार्दिक प्रणाम।

Visit to Sarvahitkarini Sabha

I learnt Lokasamgraha from Gita—
That is, the message of Sarva-hitam (good-for-all)
My in-laws had established Sarvahitkarini Sabha in 1920
I visited this Sabha in 2010—
And was overwhelmed and inspired
That my in-laws had put Lokasamgraha in practice
As a source of great inspiration, 90 years ago.

2.12.6 93 साल की होतीं बीबी

लता-सी वे कोमल थीं, स्वर्ण कांति की आभा थी चेहरे पर।
सीखने, सिखाने की इच्छा सदा थी उनमें, मैं उनकी पहली शिष्या थी।।
सदा समझा मुझको अपना उत्तराधिकारी, मैंने भी आशा निभाई थी।
उनका मुझपर था प्यार बड़ा, मुझमें था सम्मान घना।
निकट बैठ जब बातें करते, समाज-विकास का ध्यान था होता।।
याद कर महापुरुषों की महानता, उनसे शिक्षा मिलती थी।
आज उन्हें मैं अर्पित करती, अपनी श्रद्धांजलि हृदय के उद्‌गारों से।।
बहन उर्मिला

93rd Birthday of Swarna Bibi

She was soft like a creeper, she had radiance of gold on her face
She was always very fond of teaching and learning, and I was her first student
She always used to think of me as her heir, and I also fulfilled her feelings
She had great love for me, I used to respect her wholeheartedly
When we used to sit together, we used to talk about social welfare
We used to remember the greatness of great people, and tried to learn from their character
Today I offer my gratitude to her
With a heart full of feelings
Sister Urmila

2.12.7 90 वीं वर्ष गाँठ पर

परसों हमारे विवाह की वर्षगाँठ थी, आज तुम्हारा है जन्मदिन।
63 वर्ष पहले हमारा हुआ मिलन, 90 वर्ष का मिला लम्बा जीवन।।
तुमने मुझको गीता सिखाई, पढ़ाई लिखाई में खूब बढ़ाया।
सहायता-भाव, त्याग-भावना का दे उदाहरण, आगे बढ़ना सिखलाया।।
कठिन से कठिन समय में भी हिम्मत रखी प्रभुकृपा से।
मैं इसकी आभारी हूँ, बड़े प्रेम से कह रही निज अपनी बात।।

90th Birthday of Satya (Tribute by Urmila)

Two days back was our marriage anniversary and today is your birthday
Today you have become 90 and 63 years ago we got married
During this period you taught me Gita and took me ahead in studies
Keeping your example in mind I learnt how to help and sacrifice for the welfare of all
In times of difficulty never get disappointed; God is with us.
I am very grateful to you and offer my tribute.

2.12.8 बचपन में पड़ी नींव

मिट्टी, रेत के बना खिलौने, बचपन में जो खेला है।
कड़ी-धूप में पैदल चलकर पाठशाला जो पहुँचा है।।
भाई-बहन और मित्रों के बीच बैठकर, बड़े प्रेम से की पढ़ाई।
माता-पिता की आज्ञा मानी, नहीं किया अपमान कभी।।
ऐसे बच्चे आगे चलकर सुन्दर नागरिक, देश भक्त और सम्मानित होतें हैं।
बचपन की पड़ी नींव ही आगे चमत्कार दिखाती है।।
सर्वहित, परहित की रख सोच, गीता का सम्मान किया।

Childhood Foundation

(On the 90th birthday of Satya)
He used to play by making toys of sand and soil
Used to walk to school in scorching heat of Rajasthan desert
Always used to study in the company of friends, brothers and sister
He was very obedient to parents, never insulted them
Such children become good citizens and patriots
And bring honor to their country
Childhood foundation is the biggest asset which shines in the future
He used to think good of all in the spirit of the Gita.

2.12.9 बुढ़ापा

बुढ़ापा! तू ही मेरा जीवन साथी, सहायक और हितैषी है।
अन्य तो आए और चले गए, तूने मेरा संग सदा निभाया।।
सीनियर सिटिज़न बनते ही तू प्रति दिन बढ़ा, घटने का लिया न नाम।
दिशा दिखाई, विश्वास सिखाया, डर से मुझको दूर भगाया।।
कहा, "हम दोनों की मंजिल एक ही है, मत समझ तू है खड़ी अकेली"।

Old Age

Old age! You are my life companion, you help me and think good of me
Younger ages came and went, but you are always with me
From the day I became senior, everyday you are moving on, never stopping

You showed me the right path, gave confidence, and taught me - 'don't be afraid!'
"Our destination is the same, don't think you are alone in any way!"

2.12.10 मेरी चाह—अपनी 85वीं वर्षगाँठ पर

इस बढ़ती हुई अवस्था में, चाह अभी कुछ बाक़ी है।
लिया समाज से जीवन भर, खाया, पिया, पहने कपड़े।।
पढ़े लिखे, देखी दुनिया, बड़े हुए योग्य बने।
कितने बड़े उपकार हैं हमपर, सोच रहती है मन पर।।
हे ईश्वर! दिखाओ ऐसा मार्ग मुझे, ऋणी कहे न कोई मुझे।
मैं भी रहूँ प्रसन्न और समाज मुझे समझे सेवक।।

Indebtedness to Society—On My 85th Birthday

Today, I recall my life's journey
Throughout our lives, we got all the necessities of life from society
We got good education, saw the world, and got so much experience
Realizing how indebted we are to society
I pray to God, "Give me strength to repay!"
May the younger generation be inspired by our lives
To render social service.

ANU-GITA
IN THE MAHABHARATA

Re-affirming Bhagavad-Gita's Message of Good-of-all

S.P. AGARWAL & URMILA AGARWAL

ISBN: 978-81-7822-468-8

Price: ₹ 500

Most people (even in India) have not heard the name of Anu-Gita. While the format of Anu-Gita is different from that of the Gita. In the Gita there are dialogues between Krishna and Arjuna. On the ohter hand, in Anu-Gita, Krishna makes use of three ancient dialogues. Anu-Gita is divided into two parts. Part I of Anu-Gita, presents the Sanskrit-shlokas with their translation. Part II explains the main points of similarity, as well as dissimilarity, between Gita and Anu-Gita. The purpose of writing this book is to make available to English-knowing readers, an easy-to-read version of Anu-Gita. Although Anu-Gita is an important part of the Mahabharata, it has so far not been presented in a simple form to common people, with the result that most people do not even know that such a book exists. The prefix 'Anu' denotes 'after', so Anu-Gita literally means 'Gita occurring after'. In the Mahabharata, Bhagavad-Gita (or Gita for short) occurs in Parva No. 6, while Anu-Gita occurs in Parva No. 14. (In all, there are 18 Parvas in the Mahabharata).